STEWARDSHIP
for VITAL
Congregations

Anthony B. Robinson

THE
PILGRIM
PRESS
Cleveland

The Pilgrim Press, 700 Prospect Avenue East,
Cleveland, Ohio 44115-1100
thepilgrimpress.com
©2011 by The Pilgrim Press

Biblical quotations are from the *New Revised Standard Version of the Bible*, ©1989 by the Division of Christian Education of the National Council of Churches of Christ in the U.S.A., and are used by permission.

SUSTAINABLE Certified Fiber
FORESTRY Sourcing
INITIATIVE
Label applies to the text stock www.sfiprogram.org

Printed in the United States of America
on acid-free paper

Library of Congress Cataloging-in-Publication Data

Robinson, Anthony B.
  Stewardship for vital congregations / Anthony B. Robinson.
      p. cm.
  Includes bibliographical references (p.   ).
  ISBN 978-0-8298-1869-7 (alk. paper)
  1. Christian giving. I. Title.
  BV772.R59 2011
  254'.8--dc22
                                    2011002806

15 14 13 12 11   1 2 3 4 5

Contents

One

This Book:
What Is It and Who Is It For?

What Kind of Book Is This?

There are lots of books, pamphlets, programs, and resource materials available on stewardship or fund development or fundraising for churches. What kind of book is this one?

Stewardship for Vital Congregations seeks to be both theologically and biblically informed and informative *and* practically helpful. This book approaches stewardship from the standpoint of Christian faith and conviction and the insights of Scripture. It also provides specific and practical help to congregations and their leaders as they invite members and friends of the congregation they serve and lead to engage in the spiritual practice of Christian stewardship and to be part of the mission and ministry of the congregation.

In other words, this book may fly up to the ten-thousand-foot level of high concepts and faith affirmations, but it gets down to the ground where church leaders live and work to develop the financial resources that support the mission of the church. This book is more than a how-to, for it is shaped by faith's convictions, Scripture's insights and—this is especially important—an awareness of the complex and changing culture of twenty-first century North

America and the real challenges that changing culture poses for the church and its leaders. And it also offers particular strategies and "how-to's" for pastors and committees working on stewardship.

As you look at this introduction and ask "Is this book for me? Is it for us?" another way to help you answer those questions is to say what this book is not. Philosophers call this "the *via negativa*," the negative way (which isn't the same as "being negative"). Rather it is saying what something is not. Let me elaborate my basic answer to the question "What kind of book is this?" with several quick thoughts on what it is not.

This book is *not* another "stewardship program." Clergy and churches frequently receive mailings, phone solicitations, or e-blasts with the "latest," "newest," "most exciting" or "sure-to-succeed" program for raising money. "Follow these seven (three, ten, twelve) steps and we promise stupendous success!" This book isn't that program or really any "program." Why not?

Two reasons: such programs don't usually go deep enough. They don't get to the level of stewardship as a spiritual practice that changes lives. Nor do they often deeply engage the really important questions of a church's mission or purpose. The second reason for this not being another program is related to the first. Even if such a program is "successful," such success is usually neither lasting nor sustainable. It may work for one or two years, at most three, before the "magic" fades and you're looking for the next program. The approach of this book goes deeper. We aim for an approach to stewardship that forms and deepens people's faith while focusing on and furthering a congregation's core purpose or mission. We aim for something that is not a quick fix but a sustainable practice.

Another thing this book is not is a catalogue of inspirational thoughts with the implicit promise that if you sprinkle them over a congregation it will result in greater giving. Not a few stewardship resources take this tack. They offer inspiring quotes, thoughts, verses of Scripture, stories, and anecdotes. In themselves, there is nothing wrong with any of these. Moreover, I hope that you will find this book to be "inspiring," at least every now and then, and it does have a number of stories. But this book aims to be more than a catalogue of inspiring thoughts or a compendium of motivational quotations or stories. We plan to provide you a faith-based perspective on stewardship that sees stewardship as part of the church's overall task of teaching and living a particular way of life, a Christian way of life.

A third thing this book is not is a book about stewardship as a theme that relates to all of life, from care of the earth to stewarding one's own gifts and talents. To be sure, "stewardship" does imply all of this. It is a big, broad, and wonderful theme and concept rooted in the idea that all of life is a gift of God and a trust from God, with implications for care of the earth, vocational callings, and lifestyle choices. Stewardship, in the broadest sense, truly includes all of those things. But when something includes everything, there's a risk, namely, that we don't say much of anything in a particular or specific way. So this book, while fully aware of and affirming of the breadth and depth of the Christian concept of stewardship, is *primarily* about our stewardship of money. It is primarily about how congregations and their leaders can create a culture of giving and generosity that changes lives and supports the mission and ministry of the church with adequate financial resources.

Moreover, there are valid reasons for such a limited focus. For one thing Jesus spoke frequently about money. In fact, as a topic Jesus spoke of money more than any other single topic except the Kingdom of God. And Scripture as a whole addresses the matter of money and its place in our lives often. In the Book of Acts, for example, how people use money serves as a kind of barometer of their spiritual health. So though stewardship is a wonderfully large concept with a host of implications, our focus here is a more limited one: the role of money in the lives of people of faith and in supporting the mission and ministry of the church.

What kind of book is this? Let's sum up. This is *not* a book with a new, sure-fire stewardship program for you to download into your church's life. Nor is it a book of inspiring thoughts or Bible studies that will somehow magically move people to be more generous. And, finally, this is not a book about stewardship as symbol or metaphor for all of life.

What kind of book is this? It is a book that is informed by faith's convictions and Scripture's insights that will help congregations and their leaders to invite people into a way of life that makes a difference. This way of life makes a difference for individuals and families as they use and relate to money. It makes a difference for congregations as they participate in God's mission and purposes of mending a broken creation and developing the resources to support that participation.

Who Is This Book For?

People who write books like to think and hope that their books are for everyone. In reality, the target audience is usually and should be smaller. This book has several particular audiences in mind.

First, it is a book for church leaders, both clergy and lay leaders. In particular it is a book for those church leaders who are charged with leading a stewardship program, drive, or campaign. As with all the books in the Congregational Vitality series, we intend this book to give church leaders a combination of solid knowledge and practical tools to lead a particular ministry and to carry out a particular task. So if you are a lay leader or clergy person who has the job of working on, developing, and leading your church's stewardship program, this book is for you!

This book is also for you if you are a member of a board or team or committee that has something to do with developing, managing, and deploying a congregation's resources in order to accomplish its mission. It is my hope that groups like a church's governing board, council, consistory or session, or trustees will read, study, and discuss this book together as a way of furthering your own faith formation and of deepening your skills.

All too often such groups stay only at the level of the next fourteen tasks to do this month or the urgent things we have to do right now for the immediate crisis. While that is understandable, when task-driven and crisis-driven become the norm for how a church committee, board, or team operates, then "burnout" is not far off. Doing particular tasks needs always to be funded by deeper thinking, by faith formation, and by an encounter with a holy and gracious God. From such deeper wells we may draw a lasting supply of living water. So I encourage such teams or groups to use this book as a study book together for a year or a season. To aid you in such use, the book has two features. First, by and large the chapters are short, the kind of thing you can read at one sitting. Second, each chapter has "Questions for Reflection, Discussion, and Action."

A third group for whom this book is intended are those who work as staff or volunteers at a judicatory (Association, Conference, Presbytery, District, or Synod) on stewardship and fund development. For many such bodies this is a tough row to hoe these days. We're being asked to do more with less and to smile as we do! Nevertheless, you have an important role to play, not only in developing funds to support the work of the judicatory, but in assisting congregations to develop the funds they need to support their congregation's mission and ministry. This book is intended to help you, too.

I also hope that this book will be of interest to individuals, church members and Christians who want to think about the role of money in their lives, how they use money, how they can make a positive difference with their use of money, and how they may grow in the practices of generosity and sharing. All of these audiences are made up of people who share this in common: you seek to "steward," that is, manage, care for, and support the church of Jesus Christ. This book is for people who love the church (even if they quarrel with it at times), who believe in the church, and wish to see the church, in all its manifestations, flourish. (Note: I did not say "survive"; I said "flourish." There is a difference.)

Finally, this book is part of a series of books from The Pilgrim Press: The Congregational Vitality series. Our goal for the series is to help congregations of the United Church of Christ be more vital and healthy. While our first audience is churches of the United Church of Christ, we hope and believe that others, particularly of the Protestant mainline tradition will also find this book helpful and pertinent.

Who Writes This Book?

I am an ordained United Church of Christ minister, a pastor and teacher of the church. I have served four congregations, which include a diversity of types of churches. Those four included larger and smaller churches, rural and urban ones, and congregations that are primarily Anglo as well as a couple that are multicultural, multiracial, and multiethnic.

As a congregational minister I have been part of more than twenty-five annual stewardship programs, three capital fund drives, and the development and support of several planned giving programs. I am happy to report that in all those instances we have enjoyed success. Every congregation I have been privileged to serve has grown in giving (real, post-inflation dollars) and in support for its mission and ministry. Every capital drive I have been a part of has exceeded its goals. And in the planned giving area, we have helped churches to establish and grow their endowments.

In addition to this on-the-ground experience as a pastor, I have also had the privilege and opportunity to gain other kinds of experience as I have worked with a variety of congregations as a teacher and consultant. These have included all of the mainline Protestant denominations, as well as some Roman Catholic and Evangelical churches. In this work, my mission is to "Build congregations by strengthening leaders." Sometimes we have focused on stewardship, but often the themes have been church or congregational renewal, leadership development and support, or planning. I have also had the chance to speak and teach at both national and regional conferences that had a stewardship focus.

Finally, I have written a bunch of books and articles on churches, their leadership and theology, and their renewal. In several of these books, including *Transforming Congregational Culture* and *Changing the Conversation: A Third Way for Congregations* (see the Resources section at the end of the book), I have had something to say about stewardship, money, budgets, and related topics. This particular book, as already noted, is part of a series of books by The Pilgrim Press for which I have been honored to serve as general editor. All of the books in this series are intended to be the kind of book a church leader, whether clergy or lay, brand new or experienced, can pick up and *use*. So that's something about *What kind of book is this? Who this book is for?* and *Who this book is by?* Now it's your turn to reflect, talk and, act.

Questions for Reflection, Discussion, and Action

1. Do a quick word association on "stewardship." What words, thoughts, feelings pop up when you hear that word? If you are with others, make a few notes and then share and talk together.

2. Why are you reading this book? What are you hoping to get out of the experience? Be as specific as you can. If you are in a group, jot down a few notes, share and discuss your thoughts.

3. Think of one of your earliest childhood experiences of with money. What kind of experience was it (happy, painful, fun, sad, fearful, proud, etc.)? What feelings or lessons did it leave you with? Again, if you're in a group, make a few notes, share, and then discuss.

Two

Stewardship in a New Time

Adecade ago a large United Church of Christ congregation in New England **was making plans for a capital campaign.** The campaign was to coincide with the two-hundredth anniversary of the church's founding. Church leaders had in mind a two-pronged purpose for the capital drive. The first would be a major service project, conceived as something like a "birthday gift" from the church to the community. What was envisioned was the creation of a residential home for mentally challenged or developmentally disabled adults. The other aspect of the project would be a major renovation to the church building. Leaders projected a need to raise four million dollars to accomplish the two goals.

As is common practice in such capital campaigns, a consulting firm was engaged to do a financial feasibility study. After interviewing a number of individuals and small groups within the congregation the consultants returned to the leadership with their report. They said that $2.5 million would be as much as the church could possibly expect to raise in a capital drive. There simply wasn't support sufficient to meet the $4 million goal. The difficulty, according to the consultants, was twofold. First, the congregation didn't really understand the needs. Second, and potentially much more serious, those interviewed felt the church lacked an overarching sense of purpose, a sense as the new senior minister, put it, "Of what this is all about."

13

The church's leadership did not accept the recommendation of the consultants to downsize the goal to $2.5 million, but neither did they go ahead as planned with the capital drive. Rather the church's leaders settled on a third option. They decided to step back and engage the congregation in an extended process of discernment in order to come up with, or discern, a clear sense and statement of overarching purpose, "Of what this is all about." They sought to discover the purpose or mission of the church as it began its third century.

Two years later, and after many different forms and experiences of discerning together, the congregation had developed a compelling "why we are here" statement. That statement went as follows: "In every way, in every setting, we seek to nurture and experience Growth in Faith." Beyond that the statement indicated five pathways or core ministries though which this central purpose would be pursued. These were "Glorifying God through Worship, Bonding in Community, Learning the Christian Gospel and Practice, Sharing our Faith, Manifesting Enthusiasm for Service."[1]

The process of discernment was carried forward in a simple, though not simplistic, way by exploring two questions and pondering them over time in a variety of ways and settings in the life of the church. The two questions were, "Where do you sense the presence of God here?" and "Where do you sense God is asking us to go?" The questions were addressed in small groups, in sermons, in board and committee meetings, in personal prayer and in prayer groups, in adult study sessions, and in church school classes and youth group meetings. Everyone was involved. Everyone talked about the two questions and listened to what was said. As they listened to one another, they also listened for God and for what the Holy Spirit was saying through them and to them.

The sustained exploration of these two questions led, in time, to the clear statement of the congregation's overarching purpose and to the particular series of five foci or directions it envisioned for the next chapter of the congregation's life in order to more faithfully and fruitfully fulfill that purpose. When the congregation did eventually move ahead on the capital drive, it did so with a much clearer and stronger sense of the mission of the church, as well as the challenges it believed God was calling it to address and the needs they were asked to meet. The result, for the fund drive itself, was telling and dramatic. The congregation raised in excess of $10 million.

Whether a congregation is larger or smaller, this story is an instructive one. In order for the congregation to invite people to increase their giving and successfully raise money, this church needed to be able to clearly state, "Why we are here," and to articulate "what this is all about."

Moreover, it is not an accident (1) that a two-hundred-year-old congregation had lost clarity about its purpose and priorities or (2) that engaging in a deliberate and thoughtful process for discerning purpose and priorities afresh was needed and timely. Based on work with scores of congregations, it is my general observation that the longer a congregation exists the less likely it is vitally connected to a clear and compelling sense of purpose. (I use the words "purpose" and "mission" interchangeably but prefer "purpose.") There are, of course, exceptions to this generalization. Nevertheless, most congregations begin with a strong sense of purpose or mission. Over time this tends to erode. Purpose is lost or forgotten. In its place the goal becomes maintaining the organization or institutional survival, which is not a real mission or purpose, for it has turned the means into an end. Churches do not exist simply to maintain themselves. They exist to advance the realm or reign of God, proclaimed and embodied in Jesus Christ.

This particular congregation had a good and noteworthy history. It had just enjoyed a long, thirty-year pastorate. It was due, perhaps overdue, to revisit the basic questions, "What's our purpose or mission today? Are we clear about it? Can we communicate it to others in ways that are engaging, even compelling?"

Capital drives frequently present such opportunities. What I want to suggest, however, is that in our new time congregations need to be able to communicate a compelling sense of core purpose as well as their key priorities, not just for the periodic capital fund drive, but consistently and on an ongoing basis. Or to put it negatively, the challenge that many congregations encounter when they conduct a stewardship drive is that they are unable to articulate a real and compelling sense of purpose or mission. There is no "overarching sense of purpose," no clear sense or statement, to use that New England pastor's word, "of what this is all about."

In place of clarity about purpose what we often get is a survival orientation or mentality or the assumption that everyone is already clear on what the church is about and united in that purpose. When survival takes over and purpose erodes, we hear and say things like, "We need you to give if this church is going to be here in the future" or "your support is crucial if this church is going to survive." But such appeals miss more basic questions and conversations. Why should this church survive? To what end and for what purpose do we as a congregation exist? What are we trying to accomplish for

God? Part of the significance of our "new time" (a term to be unpacked more later) is that churches can no longer take for granted that people, even including their members, know or understand their core purpose or mission. Today, congregations must be more intentional and articulate about the reason for their being, what the French term *raison d'être*.

Appeals to institutional survival really work, if they work at all, only for long-time members, people who have institutional loyalty, and people who are organizational insiders. It's difficult to engage those who aren't insiders on the basis of survival or institutional loyalty–based appeals. Even long-term, historic churches (or other institutions like colleges or hospitals) need, in order to be vital, to be able to communicate their overarching sense of purpose. And they need to be able to do so in ways that capture people's interest and imagination.

Throughout this book, and particularly in this chapter, I will argue that a crucial challenge facing those leading the stewardship ministry of a congregation is for a congregation, and its leaders, to address some essential questions:

- Why are we here?
- Where do we sense God is calling us to go in the future?
- What is the "reason for our being"?
- What God-given purpose do we serve?
- Whose lives do we seek to touch or change, and in what way?
- Is there reason to believe that we, as a congregation, are accomplishing the purpose for which God has called us?

That New England congregation discovered that it could not expect to conduct a successful capital drive until it has good answers to such questions. My contention is that we cannot expect any stewardship or fund development efforts to succeed if we don't have good answers to these questions.

When we don't have good, thoughtful, and convincing answers to these questions, what happens tends to be uninspired, even deadly. Here's a thumbnail of a fairly typical version of stewardship in a congregation that hasn't struggled with and developed God-led and inspired answers to the "what this is all about" questions and is instead focused mainly on institutional survival.

One Sunday Mr. Jones gets up after the sermon and comes to the lectern. After a few moments of adjusting the microphone with attendant creaks and

16

scratches, Mr. Jones indicates that he has been asked to lead the stewardship program this year. Everything about Mr. Jones, his posture, tone of voice, and hesitations in speech, manages to communicate, "This is no fun, in fact it's really awful, but someone has to do it. I guess I got the short straw. So here I am. I don't like this any better than you do." Mr. Jones clears his throat and says,

> Well, you know how it is. Costs keep going up. Health care for our staff is more expensive this year. And it takes quite a bit of money to heat this old church. So we've looked at the budget. We're going to need 7 percent more than last year. The trustees have thought about it. We've tried to cut wherever we could. We know times are hard. We know membership is down. But we need to ask you to dig a little deeper. We'd like everyone to consider raising their pledge by 7 percent for the coming year. If we can just all think about that now and fill out our pledge cards by next Sunday, I think we'll be fine for another year. Maybe we won't have to do like we did last year just before the Annual Meeting and have that special follow-up appeal. Let's hope not. Thank you.

Pretty inspiring, isn't it? Perhaps you think I've exaggerated a bit, and maybe I have, but not much. Often, and in many congregations, this is pretty close to reality.

Let's note a couple things. First, there isn't any sense or statement of the church's purpose or mission. There's no real attempt to communicate "what this is all about," or "what God has called us to be and do as the church of Jesus Christ." Rather, what is communicated is an appeal to make the budget for another year. A budget, let us remember, is not an end or a goal. It is a means to an end. The end or goal is the church's mission or purpose. By focusing primarily on the budget, the emphasis falls on the means while the question of ends, purpose, and goals and the chance to address them has been missed. Generally, clarity about the larger goals and purpose is the source, or at least a potential source, of energy and excitement. Percentage increases in the budget occasioned by rising costs seldom generate either excitement or energy.

Second, people are given a goal (that is good!), but the goal is to give "7 percent more than last year" because the cost of a couple of key items, heating and health care, has gone up. Suppose that your annual pledge is

$5,000, while mine is $500. Suppose furthermore that we enjoy roughly the same income. This appeal to increase our giving by 7 percent means $35 for me, but $350 for you. Such budget-based appeals often end up, however inadvertently, reenforcing strong habits of weak giving for some while placing a disproportionate demand on others.

Now imagine a different church. Here another Mr. Jones gets up. He appears energetic, even excited. He says,

> I've been asked to play a role in our stewardship program this year, and I'm pleased to do that. This church means a great deal to me. One of the reasons it means so much is that this church and the faith I've been helped to grow and develop here has changed my life. In fact, in some ways I feel that I'm the "poster boy" for our church's mission. You know what our mission is, don't you? It's "Changing Lives by Growing People of Faith." In these times that's a very important mission. So many people are seeking meaning and purpose. I see strong evidence that our church is fulfilling its mission in many ways. In the next couple of weeks you'll hear from others in the congregation about just how they have seen and experienced for themselves our church Changing Lives by Growing People of Faith. You're going to hear some wonderful stories of faith in action. We think you have wonderful stories yourself. In fact, we'd like you to share those stories of changing lives and growing faith on our church's website. Here's how you can do that . . .

Mr. Jones continued,

> As we look at the year ahead, we have several really important priorities. God has put some real challenges before us. I'm not going to try to tell you all about them today. That will be developed in the weeks to come. But I do want to say this: one of the ways our church has helped me to grow in faith has been by asking me to become a more generous and giving person. I still have growing to do, but I've learned so much from so many of you about being a giving person. So that's why I'm really pleased to be a part of our stewardship ministry this year, and I hope you'll join me.

You can see in the presentation from the second Mr. Jones several key differences. (1) He's able to communicate "what it is we're all about." He clearly states the purpose or mission of the church, "Changing Lives by Growing People of Faith." (2) He indicates that this purpose has had real implications for his own life. (3) He invites others to join him, first by being part of the God's work through the church, second by sharing their own stories of changed lives and growing faith, and third by joining him in becoming generous givers. (4) (Did you notice this?) Our second Mr. Jones spoke of God. He spoke about God's work and his experience of God's presence. All of this, the church's mission and his involvement, seemed in some way to have to do with a living God. If you look back at the first Mr. Jones, one of the things that's striking is that there is really no sense of God's presence in what he says about giving or about the church. There's no God in it, only a building, a budget, and a tedious chore.

So here's my thesis about stewardship in a nutshell. Stewardship is not primarily about "making the budget" (budgets have their place and can be helpful tools in managing a church and its resources, but they aren't the point.) Neither is stewardship an appeal to "support the church," simply because people have an assumed obligation to do so. Neither "making the budget" nor "institutional obligation" are particularly inspiring or faithful, though both are often enough the basis upon which many churches conduct their stewardship program and make their appeal.

Instead, there are two crucial and related grounds upon which stewardship ministry rests in our new time. One is a reasonably clear sense and statement of the purpose, or mission, of the church. That is, the "what this is all about." And the other main point, one that is related to the first, is that stewardship is a personal spiritual practice or, as the second Mr. Jones put it, it is about becoming a more generous and giving person. Churches are in the business, so to speak, of changing lives, what some call "people-making." We are in the business of forming particular kinds of people with particular values and behaviors. Surely, generosity in spirit and with money are at the heart of that venture.

These two are really parts of one whole, but each deserves clear and distinct emphasis. This chapter will emphasize the first, the church's purpose and mission. The next chapter will emphasize the second, stewardship as spiritual practice. The stewardship ministry of the congregation is about these two things: (1) The purpose or mission of the church. What is it that God has called us to do and be? Are we passionate about that? Is it happening? And (2) stewardship ministry is about inviting each and every person to grow in the spiritual practices of generosity, of giving, of sharing. It is about creating a culture of giving in the midst of an often anxious and fearful world. We will return to this aspect and theme in the next chapter on Stewardship as a Spiritual Practice.

This is what we are up to in our stewardship ministry in the church: we are talking about our God-given, God-inspired purpose and mission as the church of Jesus Christ. And we are inviting people to grow spiritually by growing in generosity. If a church's purpose is like that of the church of the second Mr. Jones, "Changing Lives by Growing People of Faith," then these two emphases—the church's mission and personal spiritual growth—fit together as integrated parts of one whole. But both are important. Both are at the heart of stewardship in a new time for vital congregations.

How are churches to go about strengthening and focusing their sense of purpose or mission? If a congregation is unclear about its core purpose, how do leaders help a congregation to find both clarity and passion?

I suggest that it begins with your pastoral leadership. Does your minister or ministers have a sense of the purpose and mission of the church? Can they communicate it in ways that others "catch" it? If they do not have that, they need to figure it out. If they are unable to do so, your church may need different leadership. Still, this does not mean that the minister simply tells everyone what the church's purpose is or will be, nor that the minister alone answers the question of purpose. It means that anyone ordained to ministry should have, or soon acquire, a biblically shaped and theologically informed sense of the church's purpose. It means they encourage others to think about, discuss, and struggle with those themes and questions. Clergy should be able to bring Scripture and Christian theology to bear on such questions. In Appendix One, you will find a brief annotated list of Scripture and theological themes that are particularly important for congregations that seek to strengthen their sense and statement of purpose. In Appendix Two you will find some sample church purpose or mission statements from congregations with which I have worked, as well as some criteria for what, in my experience, helps to make such a statement useful and effective. Appendix Three suggests a process for a congregation that wishes to develop a sense and statement of purpose or mission.

Sometimes a church can take steps toward strengthening its sense and statement of purpose by conducting, over time, the kind of discernment process of the congregation with which we began in this chapter. Other congregations may wish to do a more focused and shorter process to get to the same end using the process in Appendix Three. Another option is to use the large group process known as "Future Search" about which information is available on the Internet. Sometimes congregations will engage consultants or facilitators who draw on other process formats. But note this well: coming up with a purpose or mission statement is only a beginning. After you develop it, you have to use it!

Important note: You may have noticed that I have written of both a "sense" and a "statement" of purpose. Both are important. If a church grows through a process to develop a statement of purpose or mission but doesn't have a strong "sense" of purpose, the purpose/mission statement won't mean much. Moreover, some congregations aren't ready to participate in such a process because levels of trust are too low or levels of conflict are too high. When that is the case leadership (pastoral and lay) can and should still seek to have and communicate a "sense" of purpose. Additionally, a "statement" of purpose is not just a cherry on top or a decoration. It must have meaning throughout the church's life and decision-making. Allocation of resources and development of ministries should be guided and disciplined by purpose.

Before I conclude this chapter and invite you to reflect on and discuss several questions, let me return briefly to a term I used in the title of this chapter, "Stewardship in a New Time." What do I mean by a "New Time"?

Many of our churches were established and learned to be and do church in the era of "North American Christendom." During that time, which started to crumble fifty years ago, there was a working partnership between the church and North American culture, by which each relied upon and enforced the other. So, for example, my elementary school day, fifty years ago, began with the Pledge of Allegiance to the flag of the United States, a reading from the Bible, and a prayer. Stores were closed on Sunday, and not much else happened on that day—except church. In countless ways, Christianity and American culture were woven together and were mutually reinforcing. It was "Christendom," which is a word that is the combination of two words, "Christianity" and "Dominion." It means Christian rule or governance or establishment. While Christianity was not legally established in the United States, it was in many ways culturally established. By and large, that's over now. If you want read a fuller account of these changes and what they mean I suggest my books *Transforming Congregational Culture* or *Changing the Conversation: A Third Way for Congregations.* I also suggest you look at Appendix Four of this book and the document there titled "Then and Now." "Then and Now" captures very well the "Then" of Christendom as well as the "Now" of a new time.

21

Our New Time can be described in short form in the following way: In twenty-first-century North America, we live in an officially secular, religiously pluralistic, ethnically and culturally diverse society. During Christendom we lived in a culturally Christian society, dominated by the Protestant mainline churches and denominations and with a higher degree of ethnic and cultural homogeneity. The implications of this shift for churches are many and complex. For a more complete exploration see my two books cited above.

For stewardship, as well as other aspects of the church's life, one way to sum this up is that today, in our new time, people come to and participate in churches less from *a sense of obligation* (it's what is expected of me) and more from *a sense of motivation* (I'm looking for something even if I'm not quite sure what it is). In the period of North American Christendom we could count on people feeling a sense of obligation to be a part of the church and to provide some financial support. While some of that still exists, by and large churches today need to address what motivates people to seek a church and be a part of a community of faith. In order to do so, churches in our new time need increasingly to be clear about their purpose, to communicate that purpose effectively, and to fulfill that purpose fruitfully.

Questions for Reflection, Discussion, and Action

1. Do you feel your congregation has a strong, clear sense of its purpose or mission?

2. Does your congregation have a succinct, compelling purpose or mission statement? Is that statement known by all and "owned" by both leaders and members of the congregation?

3. If you do not have a strong sense and statement of "what this is all about," how might you go about getting to the place where you do? Who should give leadership in that work? How should the pastor(s) be involved? How should the congregation be involved? How can you seek God's will for your congregation and its mission at this time?

4. If there is no formal "mission statement," can your stewardship team, in concert with pastoral leadership, express "why we are here" as a church in a provisional way, and then invite others into that conversation?

Three

Stewardship: A Spiritual Practice

In the previous chapter I argued that the stewardship program of a congregation has a dual focus. One emphasis, the subject of that chapter, is the overall mission and ministry of the church. Who are we? What has God called us to do? Do we have a strong sense of our purpose or mission? Can we communicate our purpose or mission effectively?

Another way to put this is that stewardship is not separate from the overall and ongoing life of the congregation. If the congregation has a strong sense of purpose and identity, if there is enthusiasm for that mission, if the various aspects of the congregation's life (worship, education or formation, outreach) are informed by that sense of purpose, then stewardship has a strong foundation upon which to build. If, on the other hand, a congregation has little or no clear sense of purpose or mission, if there is little capacity to articulate purpose, if other aspects of the life of the church are in maintenance mode, then it's difficult to suddenly light a fire for stewardship. Michael Durall, in his fine book *Creating Congregations of Generous People*, makes this point clearly: "You cannot take a congregation that is somnolent for eleven months of the year and make members wildly enthusiastic about giving during the twelfth."[1]

Stewardship has to be seen in context, the larger context of congregational health and vitality. For a larger picture of what that means and how to get there, readers may wish to consult the first book in this series, my *Leadership for Vital Congregations*.

So one focus of stewardship is the mission and ministry of the church, knowing what our purpose and mission are, being focused on that purpose in our varied programs and ministries, and being able to communicate our purpose and story.

There is a second equally important focus: stewardship as a spiritual practice, a practice of growing in generosity, in giving, and in sharing with open hands and hearts. Churches exist to change lives. One of the core ways that churches change lives is by helping people to be and become more trusting, generous, and giving. These are spiritual practices. They have to do with our sense of who we are and how we exist in the world, of who God is, whether we can trust God and whether we are able to give and commit ourselves to purposes and meanings larger than our self. All of these are aspects of what is central to the life and being of churches, namely faith.

So when we engage in our stewardship program, we are not doing something peripheral, an extra, or an onerous add-on to be gotten through as quickly as we can and with as little notice as possible. Stewardship is not simply about "funding" or "meeting" the budget as if it were a purely bureaucratic or managerial nuisance or necessary evil. No, stewardship is right at the heart of things! It is right at the heart of changing lives and growing people of faith. In fact, stewardship, generosity, and our relationship to money are right at the heart of issues of personal transformation.

In his book *The Life You Can Save*, Peter Singer relates the story of Tom Hsieh and his wife, Bree. Together they made a commitment to live on less than the U. S. median annual income ($46,000 then) and give the rest away, mostly to Christian organizations helping the poor in developing countries. "Hsieh says that whether or not his giving has saved the lives of others, it has saved his own: 'I could easily have lived a life that was boring and inconsequential. Now I am graced with a life of service and meaning.'"[2]

Over and over again I have seen people grow and change in profound ways as they struggled with giving and as they grew in their giving. Few other single aspects of the church's life hold the possibility for personal growth in relationship with God and for personal transformation as this area of stewardship. For this reason, I become concerned about ordained leaders who take an approach of distance or lack of interest in stewardship. That would be like a farmer purposefully refusing to farm some of his best land or most fertile soil. True, ordained leaders have to be thoughtful about how they go about this. They must have integrity. But for clergy or churches not to see the opportunities for growth in faith, hope, and love that exist here is to have missed, arguably, the heart of the matter.

At the conclusion of chapter 1, I posed a question that invited you to recall an early memory you had in relation to money. As we turn to stewardship as a spiritual practice, let me start with such a memory of my own as a way of telling my own stewardship story.

If I were to dredge around for a while I would probably find an earlier memory of money than this one, but this is one that comes readily to mind and stands out. I was eight years old and had just begun my first job. I was to deliver a little newspaper known as a "shopper." It was all ads, mostly for local stores or from individuals selling this or looking for that. A bundle of two hundred copies was dropped off at my home on Wednesday at midday. After school my job was to deliver them door to door. For this I received the princely sum of $1.00, which was tucked into a three-by-five manila envelope and stuck under the binder twine that held the bundle of papers together. This was the first of a series of jobs I had as a kid, jobs that included selling donuts door to door, delivering the morning paper, flipping hamburgers, and yard work for neighbors.

When I proudly displayed my first dollar from the shopper route to my father he suggested that we frame it and hang it on the wall of my room—my first dollar earned! Back then it was not uncommon to see a framed bill in stores and businesses, the first dollar they had earned. So my dad suggested we do that, and I agreed, though I'm not sure I was that thrilled to put my entire first paycheck into effective cold storage. There were, as I think back on it, many messages to me about money in that first framed dollar bill. One was that money was important. It could be framed and hung on the wall. Another was that my earning money was also important. Clearly, this was cause for taking note and being proud. I got the message that it was important for me to "make" money and that doing so had something to do with my worth. Not long after my dad would haul me off to the Federal Home Saving and Loan bank to establish my first savings account, which amplified the messages about money and added another: better to save than spend.

All of these messages about money—that it was important, that my "making" money was good, and that saving money was valuable—are I think good messages, but each one has the potential to go bad. At times in my life I have struggled with the shadow side of these messages about money. Though I decided early on that simply making money or lots of it wasn't my goal in life, I still have struggled at times with money being a gauge and indicator of my value. I have felt a keen responsibility to "produce" an income and support my family. Again, not a bad thing, in many ways a good one, but like most virtues it can flip over into a vice. Valuing money and work did at times mean that I saw my personal worth bound too closely to my income. The virtue of saving money can also flip over into miserliness.

This was the mixed bag of raw material I brought to the church and to God when it came to money. While my family also instilled in me virtues of doing my part, of service and responsibility, I don't recall a lot of direct teaching or encouragement in the practice of generosity as expressed in financial giving. As a young adult and a student my own giving in church tended to be what I found in my wallet on a Sunday morning, which often wasn't much! I would put the dollar or two that was there into the plate as it passed. Despite being raised in the church, I hadn't thought much about stewardship, the use of money, or giving beyond the values noted above. Though my seminary education did include a lot of emphasis on global poverty and wealth, the poor in the Bible and related themes, nothing was said about personal stewardship, generosity as a spiritual practice, or stewardship as something I would be involved in as a minister.

That all changed when I became a minister and went to serve my first church. Suddenly I found myself having a role in the annual stewardship program. Moreover, that first congregation decided not long after my arrival and with my support to undertake a capital drive to enlarge and upgrade its building. I realized that I had lots to learn and a steep learning curve. I needed to learn how to go about playing my part in a stewardship program and giving leadership in the pending capital drive, which was also my first experience of this kind of thing. I was twenty-eight years old, married with one child. My annual income, and I was the sole income earner for our family at that time, was $8,900.

You don't learn everything you need to know about ministry in seminary, nor should you expect to. I had the wits and good fortune to find a good teacher in the area and practice of stewardship. He was a longtime associate minister at a larger congregation in a nearby city. Learning of his reputation, I made an appointment to discuss the whole business of stewardship and fundraising and to explore the possibility that he might work with us on our upcoming capital drive.

This minister, John, did indeed have a wealth of experience and knowledge to share with me and with my congregation. We hired him to work with us. He proposed to me and to our congregation what he called "the modern tithe." The modern tithe was the idea that we were challenged and encouraged to give 5 percent of our personal income to God's work through the church and 5 percent to God's work through other programs, agencies, or charities that we believed were doing God's work in the world.

Part of the beauty of this "modern tithe" was that it was pretty simple, at least in one respect. That is, the real dollar implications were easy to determine and spell out. 5 percent translated to $1.00 per week per thousand dollars of annual income. So in our case, 5 percent to God's work through the church meant $8.90 a week, with another $8.90 a week to other programs or ministries beyond the congregation. John said that these were "challenge pledge goals" and guidelines. Not everyone would be able to give at that level right away, but we were encouraged to work toward these goals.

My wife and I took a deep breath and decided to make the commitment. We pledged 5 percent to God's work through the church. I don't think we quite got there initially on the additional 5 percent giving to other places. Overall, we probably started at about a 7 percent to 8 percent total giving. But that was a big change with a host of implications.

One of the implications was that in being this intentional about our giving it became a part of our life. And, as a corollary, we started doing monthly budgets for the first time in our married lives. Now our charitable giving was right up there with other major expenses like food, gas, and clothing on the family budget sheet. (Churches can use this as an opportunity to teach basic money management principles, which are important and in a society of consumerism and credit nearly countercultural.)

In retrospect I saw that three important things had happened. We had gotten on the path to being more generous and doing so in a systematic and regular way. It became part of our lives. Second, we became a good deal more intentional about managing money overall. As I said, we created a budget for the first time, recorded our expenses, and kept track of where the money was going. This, particularly for a young family, was important. It helped us to avoid what has happens to too many young families these days, incurring an onerous level of personal indebtedness. Third, this practice put me and us in a position to speak with confidence to the congregation as a whole about stewardship and giving.

After my childhood lessons about the value of money and the importance of me producing and providing, these early lessons in stewardship were really important, even life-transforming. They helped to avoid the shadow side of the early lessons by learning to give money away, by learning to be generous. In doing this, I learned something very important, namely, the only real way to have "enough" is by giving generously. It seemed that the loud, blaring voice of the culture (a generally affluent culture) said, "NEVER ENOUGH, NEVER ENOUGH, NEVER ENOUGH!" No matter how much you made it would never be enough. I noticed, in fact, that those who had or "made" the most money seemed most easily prey to this anxiety that they would not have enough. Somehow getting or having more didn't take away the anxiety about money, not for me, not for others. The only thing that did silence the chant of "never enough" was, paradoxically, learning to give money away freely. Over time we developed the practice of generous giving and it has shaped my life and made me a better person. Honestly, I shudder to think what kind of person I would be today if I had not been encouraged, asked, and invited by the church to learn the spiritual practices of stewardship and generosity.

A number of years later, it was stewardship time again, at another church. The year was 2002 and church leaders were nervous. As the 1990's ended in Seattle the dot.com bubble had burst, putting a big dent in the local economy. Then came 9/11/2001 and the big dent began to look like a major wreck as the stock market fell and employment went south (literally and figuratively). Despite these unfavorable economic indicators, the church council envisioned growth in church ministries, program, and budget. This was not without some basis. The church was vital and both membership and attendance were growing. Still, church leaders were nervous about the goals they proposed.

I listened carefully to the discussion. A week later I wrote my column for our newsletter with the following message:

> "Gentle, we must be gentle about this," said our very able budget chair, Patricia B. We nodded our agreement. "Gentle, yes, gentle. You must be cautious and sensitive in talking about money." The proposed budget was before the church council and we were wondering how in the world we would meet the budget, and how we could get people on board. "Gentle" was the watchword.
>
> I understand it. I support it. And yet, I wonder, is it really that hard? Are we making this more difficult than it has to be? Do we really need to be so cautious? I got my stewardship education twenty-five years ago at my first church. A consultant we asked to help us with our stewardship and capital drive gave us a challenge. "I suggest," he said, "that you commit yourselves to a goal of giv-

ing 5 percent of your personal income to God's work through the church. If you start with the biblical tithe of 10 percent, pledging 5 percent to the God's work through the church leaves you 5 percent for other causes, charities and the like. Besides," he continued, "5 percent is easy to figure, a dollar a week for each $1000 of annual income."

So starting then and ever since, that's what Linda and I have done. It's been freeing in its simplicity. We do 5 percent to the church. No matter what. When we started all those years ago, was it easy? No and yes. No, we had two kids and one not very big income. It seemed challenging. But it was, and in another sense, also easy. We just did it. Figured it out and made our commitment. Other things adjusted. I've heard it said that "True freedom is found in obedience." That's kind of been our experience. We feel pretty free about this. We don't worry about it too much. We just do it. And other things adjust. And in the course of doing this, we have discovered the joy of being generous.

I said a few other things in that letter to the congregation. But what's important was that that I could draw on my own experience and practice. I could invite others to join us in a practice and way of living in which we had discovered meaning, joy, and freedom. I didn't share so personally and directly with the congregation every year. In fact, I had been at that church twelve years at that point, when I did speak this candidly and directly. My point is not to trumpet one's own giving. Certainly we should not brag or boast. I hope I didn't. But there is a time, thoughtfully and deliberately, to share your story, your own testimony. I did that and felt on pretty solid ground. I had learned to be a generous giver. I had grown in that practice and in my faith. I had seen others grow too. Without being boastful, I did feel good about that and wanted to share it.

Can the church work with God to change and transform lives? Can inviting people into stewardship as a spiritual practice be one of the ways our lives are transformed?

In Barbara Brown Taylor's fine little book *Speaking of Sin: The Lost Language of Salvation,* she writes of how we understand sin and salvation these days and how this takes on life and substance in three different types of churches she has experienced. Her helpful discussion of sin and of types of churches provides a way for me to build on my own experience with money and giving and connect it to the large questions of what churches are up to and whether and how they change lives.

In sum, Taylor says "sin" seems today to be interpreted in three different ways, three different metaphors. One metaphor for sin is a medical one. Here sin seems to be thought of as illness, an illness we all share. "In the medical model," she writes, "the basic human problem is not called sin but sickness." And, "when sickness is substituted for sin, then illness becomes the metaphor for human failing. We receive diagnosis instead of judgment, treatment instead of penance. The medical model and metaphor give rise to a particular form of church, church as clinic." There sin-sick patients receive "sympathetic care for the disease they all share." But it is, for the most part, palliative care. That is, no one expects people to be cured, and "such churches subscribe to a kind of no-fault theology in which no one is responsible because everyone is."[3]

When it comes to stewardship the congregations that have adopted sin as sickness, with its no-fault theology and church-as-clinic, tend not to challenge people when it comes to growing in giving and generosity. Instead, such churches are likely to make excuses for people, sometimes even before making excuses for themselves. "Well, you know lots of people are on fixed incomes." "It's a tough economy right now." "People here really have to struggle to get by." These things may or may not be true. Usually there is both truth and un-truth to them. But my point is that in such churches we expect little, and we get it. We are very reluctant to ask, to challenge, to invite. We are quick to excuse our strong habits of weak giving and quick to make and accept the various excuses that people have for not growing in the practices of stewardship, generosity, and sharing. Such congregations, as Taylor notes, are not ones where anyone is getting better, where lives are being changed, or where faith is being deepened. We may offer a great deal of compassion and sympathy. We do not offer a challenge.

A second type of church in Taylor's typology tends to understand sin not as sickness but as crime. Here the metaphor and framework is not a medical one but a legal one. Sinners are law-breakers. If the theology of the former model tends toward no-fault and no-responsibility, this one tends toward full-fault, and in such churches it is not uncommon for sin and sinners to be "named out loud, along with punishments appropriate to their crimes."[4] In terms of stewardship, the church that understands sin as crime and church as a courtroom is likely to set fixed and demanding standards, to lift up and value those who meet them, and to castigate or shame those who do not. It may be true that churches that tilt this direction put more of their emphasis on other types of sin, whether sexual or doctrinal, than on giving to the church, but still the point is that the metaphor and approach here is a punitive or shaming one. Sometimes it seems that these are the only two alternatives churches can imagine: lax or harsh, understanding to a fault or demanding in the extreme. Many mainline and theologically liberal congregations will opt for understanding to a fault if the only other option is harsh or punitive.

But there is, according to Taylor, another way of thinking about sin. And there is another kind or type of church. In this framework, sin is neither sickness nor lawlessness. It is real and we are responsible, but it is not simply our doing alone or something for which we are on the hook alone. Rather sin is, in essence, "wrecked relationship." It is "wrecked relationship with God, with one another, with the whole created order. Sometimes we cause the wreckage; sometimes we are simply trapped in it." Sin in this understanding is broken relationship, while salvation is the healing and restoration of relationship. Thus the cardinal sin associated with money, greed, or avarice turns out to have as much to do with isolation and broken relationships as it does with money.

The kind of church that understands sin as "wrecked relationship," Taylor describes as "church as community-of-human-transformation." "Such a church calls individuals to take responsibility for what is wrong in the world—beginning with what is wrong with them—and to join with other people who are dedicated to turning things around."[5]

When this is applied to stewardship, it can help us see that what we are working on in relation to money and how we use it is often about relationships and broken relationships in need of healing. How we use and treat money has a lot to do with our relationships, with God, with others, and with ourselves. Hoarding money or giving only token amounts grudgingly is a sign of our brokenness and fear. It is a sign of our break with a gracious God and of our break with our fellow human beings, some of whom are trapped in poverty and want. Likewise, spending impulsively or compulsively is another indication of wrecked relationship. When we take responsibility for our sin and work on the world's brokenness, starting with our own, then we begin to develop a personal practice or stewardship and generosity that has profound meaning for our relationship with God and with our fellow human beings. Moreover, the great chasm that exists in our world between the rich and the poor may be bridged and in some measure healed as we learn and grow in the practice of generous giving and sharing.

I want to be part of a church that is, or is working to be, a "community-of-human transformation," one where we avoid the unhelpful extremes of either making peace with sin (church-as-clinic) or where sin is turned into a crime and sin and sinners are pounded into the ground (church-as-courtroom). In the churches that see themselves to be in the business of transformation and changing lives, how we relate to money, how we use money, and how we grow in the practice of generosity is all about transformation, all about growing in faith and community.

Michael Durall begins his book with a distinction that makes a fitting conclusion to this chapter. "A great deal of difference distinguishes asking people for money and creating congregations of generous people. Asking people for money eventually becomes routine, even tedious. But creating congregations of generous people is an engaging, rewarding endeavor that takes on ever more meaning with passing time."[6] Stewardship is a spiritual practice, one that like other spiritual practices, has the potential to change us, to heal us, and to deepen our faith and our lives.

Questions for Reflection, Discussion, and Action

1. What is your personal stewardship story? What lessons have you learned about money, about giving, about stewardship? Who have been your teachers? What's been helpful to you and what has proven unhelpful?

2. Discuss the connection between your money and your life as you see it and experience it.

3. What was an experience of giving and generosity in your own life that was meaningful for you and by which you were, at least in some measure, changed or transformed? This may be in or outside the church.

4. When a congregation has shrouded money with secrecy, what steps can you imagine for creating a more open, joyous, and encouraging culture of giving?

Four

Rekindle the Gift of God that Is in You

Often when I work with congregations and their leaders and the focus is on boards or committees, people complain of diminished energy or what we call "burn out." "People don't have energy for the stuff that needs to be done," someone will complain. Or, "The tasks seem endless, but time is in short supply." Or, "It's so hard to get people involved." Sometimes these problems have to do with our efforts to inhabit structures or organizational models that no longer quite fit either the mission of the church today or the world in which we live. This may lead to useful efforts to "right-size" or to "restructuring."

But at least sometimes remedies and responses to the "energy crisis" don't require a wholesale reorganization, but rather a deeper grounding of the work we are doing. Or, as Paul put it to his young protégé and budding church leader, Timothy, "Rekindle the gift of God that is in you." (2 Tim. 1:6) Go deeper. Find the fire. Reach to the depths where God has touched you and where your forebears, Eunice and Lois (in Timothy's case), planted the gift and fire of faith within you.

I often suggest to church leaders that when people on boards and committees seem to have little energy for the work, the problem may be that people are functioning at the level of seemingly endless tasks. Meeting agendas resemble to-do lists. Lacking is deeper grounding in the stories of faith and the fire of encounter with the holy God.

Picture a bell curve on a page. It sweeps upward to something like the top of the bell and then sweeps downward again. Draw such a bell curve or image one on a page before you. At the lower left write the words "myth" and "story." Midway up the ascending left hand curve write the word "Strategies." Then just before you get to the top of the curve put the word "Tasks."

The takeaway is simple. Often in church boards, committees, and teams we operate only at the task level. Our agenda is a list of tasks that have to be planned and for which we have to get people to volunteer. We are already too late on this one. We are "behind the 8-ball" on that one. Someone says, "We can't forget . . ." and yet another task, job, or assignment is added to the list. Just operating at the task point on the curve is a recipe for burnout and decline, which is why "Tasks" appears just before the curve tops out and heads downward.

In order for the "Tasks" to have meaning and for us to bring real energy to them, we have to move back down on the curve to a deeper level, to the level marked "Myth" and "Story." (By "myth" here I do not mean falsehood or fairy tale; I mean something suggested by the words of the novelist Thomas Mann, who is said to have described a "myth" as "that which never was but always is.") When Paul wished to encourage Timothy he did not push him forward, not yet anyway, but back. He directed Timothy to the faith and example of his grandmother and mother. He encouraged Timothy to remember when Paul had himself laid his hands upon Timothy, conferring power and the Holy Spirit. Go deeper, said Paul.

So many groups in the church become task groups alone, without grounding their work more deeply in the great stories and truths of the faith. So I encourage a couple of things. The worship of the church is the time in a congregation's life when we hear and tell the deep stories and when we encounter the living God. If there's an energy crisis in the church, you may need to take a look at worship. Is worship an experience of being in the presence of God (or only an experience of being with one another)? Does the preacher bring and declare a "Word from the Lord"? Is the service rich in song and symbol? Is the prayer real and heartfelt?

Sometimes people who are trying to serve on the church's boards, committees, or teams don't make worship a priority, which is sort of like trying to take off for a morning hike without breakfast, or playing in a game without practice or conditioning. It's important to be clear here. It's important to say clearly and repeatedly: "Worship is the beating heart of the church." From this beating heart blood flows to the organs and extremities. If the heart is beating very faintly or if people are failing to get in touch with the heart of things, all else suffers and is depleted.

Beyond stressing the need for meaningful and powerful worship as essential to the life of the believer and the church, I also encourage boards, committees, and teams to "fund" their work from the myth and story level by making adult faith formation experience a part of their board's life and work. What does that look like? It may mean starting a meeting with serious (and joyful) study of Scripture, which is not the same as a perfunctory "devotional." It may mean spending a brief time checking in with one another and then being in a time of prayer in which people's actual needs and authentic joys are lifted up before God.

Or it may mean that the board or team reads an article or a chapter from a book that is relevant to their area of ministry. It's helpful if someone from the group, or a pastor, has taken time to prepare to reflect on the material and plan some teaching process or experience for the group. Over the years I have found the practice of working through a good book together, one that relates to the board's work, to be of great value. It means that people who come to the meeting are not just asked to give, but given permission to receive as well, which is sort of how life works (try only breathing out for a while and see how it works for you!) You want to be able to say to people who are called to serve on boards that part of what they can expect is that they will grow in their faith and understanding because part of the experience of each such group is an adult faith formation component. Consider the books in this series (Vital Congregations) as potential study books. Those who lead study and discussion need to be carefully selected and well-prepared.

This is a longish introduction to what I want to do in this chapter, which is go to that myth and story level of our faith as it pertains to stewardship. In this chapter I want to rekindle our collective fire by turning to Scripture's stories and to core theological convictions. Often in stewardship or other areas in the life of the church, we do turn to Scripture, but with a kind of "proof-texting" or "cite-and-run" mentality. We seem to feel an obligation to throw in some Scripture texts or theological thoughts, but engagement is superficial. Further, we seem to assume that if we do so it means that we have covered our bases or that by some magic simply citing Scripture will make a difference. I'm not so sure that's true. What I'm after here is more than "covering the base." It is deeper. It is encounter with God through God's word. This is what rekindles the fire.

I have chosen six stories or passages from Scripture. That number could easily be doubled, but this is supposed to be a short book, so we will settle for six. For each I will invite and trust you to read the cited story in your Bible. Then I will provide some background, commentary, and interpretation, followed by some key "takeaways" as well as questions for you to reflect upon and discuss. (Instead of being at the end of the chapter the questions here are with each story.) After we have worked with these six texts, I will conclude this chapter with a brief affirmation of relevant core theological convictions, particularly relating to the time and experience in worship known as "the Offering."

Genesis 12:1–4a, "Setting Out"

If the first eleven chapters of Genesis provide a kind of prehistory and prelude, with accounts of creation, human origins and vocation, human sin and violence, the flood and the Tower of Babel, Genesis 12 marks the beginning of God's work to create a people and to redeem and restore creation. God begins with one man and one woman, Abraham and Sarah. Even God has to start somewhere! God calls Abraham (currently Abram; he will get his longer name a little later) and Sar'ai (she will become Sarah later) to "Go from your country and your kindred and your father's house to the land I will show you."

There are two things that are especially notable here. Abram and Sar'ai are instructed to leave a lot, everything more or less, behind. They are to leave country, extended family and parental home behind. That is to say, they are called to leave behind their known world. And for what? Well, that is not entirely clear. The destination is hidden. They are headed to, says the Lord, "a land I will show you."

In some sense this story is singular and unique, the story of Abram and Sar'ai, the father and mother of God's people. In another sense, however, this story is one that is also our own. Surely for many of us there have been times of "setting out" into the unknown and leaving behind places of comfort and security. In a deeper or more symbolic sense, life has a way of taking away our known worlds and confronting us with strange new ones. For example, we leave the world of our parents' home for some new land called college or work, military or volunteer service. We leave the land known as "single life" for marriage or partnership. We leave the life we create as a couple for a new land with a baby's crib and diapers and a saving account for college. We leave one kind of work and set of skills and set out to learn new ones. For people of faith, this dynamic has something to do with God. We perceive God to be at work here. We don't just leave; we are compelled. We don't just travel, we have been called. Somehow, in some way, the journey is in response to a word, a presence, a summons, or a call.

In his book *A Place for You*, Paul Tournier writes that "the task of mature living consists in two things: (1) Finding a Safe Place for yourself, (2) Leaving that Safe Place in a new venture."[1] "Of course," comments Walter Brueggemann, "that means that one is never safe for long but always between places."[2] If this dynamic, finding a safe place and setting out in a new venture, is at the core of the experience of God's people and of the life of faith, it means among other things that our God is one who calls us "out of our comfort zone." I don't know about you, but that has been my experience of God and of growing in faith. Growing in faith often (always?) happens as I am called out from my "comfort zone" into a place or to people or to a challenge that isn't already known or completely comfortable.

So this key episode in the entire biblical story begins just this way. Abram and Sar'ai, our forebears in our faith, the mother and father of us all, are called to leave the known world behind and to set out to an unknown place. If there is a good bit of discomfort in this, that is however not all there is. There is also a promise of God's presence. God promises to be with them, and in such times and ventures undertaken in and by faith God promises to be with us. So, to Abraham and Sarah God promises, among other things, "I will bless you, and make your name great, so that you will be a blessing." Abraham and Sarah travel under a sign and under protection. They have been marked by the Lord's blessing. Trust this and go, says the Lord.

Some Takeaways to Ponder

Here are some things that we might take away from this primal story of our faith, some that pertain to stewardship.

1. God often works with us by calling us "out of our comfort zone." This happens, particularly, perhaps, in the area of stewardship of money. We are asked, invited, to do something that is uncomfortable, something that calls us to stretch, to risk and to trust in a power and love greater than our own. Reflect on and share a time when you were "called out of your comfort zone." What happened? What did you learn?

2. As God's people we have been blessed. That is, we have known the Lord's love, presence, and grace. But we have been blessed in this way not to keep it to ourselves, but that we may be a "blessing" to others, which is what

God said to Abram and Sar'ai. In some ways, this is a pretty fair summation of what it means to be the church. That is, we are a people who have been blessed in order that we might be a blessing to others, indeed, to all people. Reflect on how you and your church have been blessed. How are you called to, able to, be a blessing to others and to your community?

Deuteronomy 26:1–11, Remember Your Story

The setting of the Book of Deuteronomy is that of a crucial transition point in the story of biblical Israel. In Deuteronomy the people stand at the brink of the Promised Land, at the bank of the Jordan River. The long journey in the wilderness, and its time of testing, challenge, and learning is behind them. Before them, on the other side of the Jordan, lies the new land, "a land flowing with milk and honey." Deuteronomy is an extended pause at this transition point. It is made up of a long sermon, or series of sermons, from Israel's leader, Moses, who speaks to the people of the meaning of their journey and of this transition from wilderness to a new and promised land.

On the one hand, it is certainly a glad time. A journey, a hard journey, has been completed. On the other, there are new and different challenges ahead. In the wilderness the people knew in a daily way their dependence upon God, who provided for them. In the new land, a land that has abundant resources where they would settle and build homes, there lay a new danger: that they would come to think of the land and its blessing not as gift, but as possession and something they own rather than as gracious gift and trust from God. Furthermore, in the new land there is the risk that the people will come to think of the land and its resources as that to which they are entitled. A slightly different way to put this is that amid the blessing and bounty of their new situation they might forget. They might no longer remember who they are, God's people who have been blessed to be a blessing to others. And they will forget their story, a story of grace and deliverance.

So in Deuteronomy 26 Moses gave the people instructions for a thank offering that they were to offer at the first and subsequent harvests. They were to take the first of the fruits of their harvest to the temple and offer them to God in order that they remember the source of the land and of its blessings. While they have worked to till the land and harvest the fruit, it is not all their doing, not by a long shot. The land is a gift and a trust from God. The very process of planting and harvest is a gift, the source of which lies in God's mysterious and gracious creation. By participating in this annual thank offering the people were to remember who they are and whose they are. They are not entitled. The land is not their possession. They are recipients of gift and grace and the land is a partner, and trust, held in a relationship.

Not only are they to remember who and whose they are; they are to remember and tell their story, the story of their deliverance from slavery and bondage in Egypt and their journey to freedom and a promised land. So, beginning in verse 5, that story is recited and given to them. It begins with "a wandering Aramean" (that would be Abraham), includes the Exodus, and concludes with the Promised Land. As the people make their offering they are to remember and to retell this story, their story and God's story.

Takeaways

1. Though we work, this does not mean that all that we have or receive is because of our work alone. Nor does it mean that what we have is "our due." We too are recipients of gift and grace, whether land and resources or brain power and knowledge. What we have is not our "entitlement"; it is a blessing, one that brings with it responsibility. In a world where it seems many do feel entitled, we in the church have a different perspective. We are recipients of gift and blessing who are expected to responsibly use as well as share that which has been entrusted to us. The previous sentence, by the way, is a pretty fair definition of "stewardship."

2. Knowing and telling our story is important, and forgetting or amnesia is always a danger. "Our story," includes the biblical story of slavery and freedom, death and new life in Christ. It also includes the story of the church throughout the ages and of our particular congregation. And it includes the story of our particular family and kin. What stories root or ground you and inform your stewardship?

Malachi 2:13–17, Godly Offerings

Malachi is the last book of the Old Testament. The name "Malachi" means "messenger." The message of this messenger is that God's people need to clean up their act. Interestingly, their offerings to God are a sign and symbol of how things have gone awry in that relationship. Malachi minces no words in telling the people that they have "polluted the altar of God." "When you offer blind animals in sacrifice, is that not wrong? And when you offer those that are lame or sick, is that not wrong?"

Since we do not ordinarily offer animals to God, this may sound weird to us. But if we translate and adjust a little bit, it might be something like this: Malachi might say to folks today, "You bring your offering to the Food Bank, but look what you are bringing. You aren't bringing fresh things. You are bringing out of date, packaged food you don't want, some that have been on your shelves forever. Instead of bringing protein-rich foods, eggs or chicken, you are bringing day-old donuts and boxes of cheap mac and cheese, and in cartons that are squashed or torn. And then you have the audacity to complain that God, that the poor don't appreciate your lavish generosity. Give me a break!"

Or Malachi might say, "You are protesting about how much your church is asking you to give. You are whining about being poor or having such big bills. But, listen, where did you go on your vacation last year? Right, you went to Mexico. Or you have heavy bills, but check out that big, new TV you have hanging in your family room. Stop your complaining, knock off your whining, and do the right thing. Bring to the Lord an honest, whole-hearted and generous gift, and then you will see what the Lord can do" (see Mal. 3:10). Try it, give 5 percent or 10 percent to the church this year, and you'll be astonished at the things that your church can do to redeem a broken world, to mend a torn creation. You'll be amazed at what will happen when, instead of whining, you do the right thing. Sometimes we too complain about God or the church, but have we truly given God our best?

Takeaways

1. There is an intrinsic relationship between our giving and our hearts (or the inner truth of our lives). When our heart is in the right place, then our offering and our giving will be also. On the other hand, diminished, depleted, or distorted offerings or giving are a sign that our relationship with God is not in a good place. What does your offering say about your relationship with God?

2. Notice that for God's people our charitable giving is not just "giving." It is "offering." That is, while our gifts may be distributed to help those in need and do God's work in the world, it is first of all an "offering" to God. Does that change things? Does it make a difference that our giving, in the church, is an "offering to God"? What difference does that suggest to you or make for you?

Matthew 7:24–33, First Things First

You may remember that in the previous chapter I cited the budget committee chairperson at my church who said that our watchword should be "gentle." "We must be gentle about this," she said in referring to seeking pledges. I pretty much feel like saying that to Jesus quite often and especially in reference to this passage. Neither here nor elsewhere, when the subject is money, does Jesus appear to be particularly gentle or even tactful. What he is instead is direct and challenging. Listen! "No one can serve two masters. . . . You cannot serve God and wealth." Make up your mind. Choose your priority, says Jesus.

My hunch is that many people then and many of us now might say, "Well, I don't exactly *serve* money or wealth." And that may be true. Maybe we make some, spend some, save some, and give some. We use money. We have money. But do we serve it? We think not. Jesus isn't so sure. He recognizes here and elsewhere that money is a strange and powerful thing. We may say it's not really a big deal to us. He's telling us, warning us, that it may be a far bigger deal than we would like to think or admit. Many have discovered this. Somehow, they don't control money. Money controls them.

Over the years in the church I've noticed that some of our most energetic, exercised, and conflictual times have to do with money. I have noticed that money can strain family relationships and even destroy them. I have noticed that people sometimes do things for money that they live to regret. Money *is* powerful, and, though we may wish to think and tell ourselves otherwise, it might be wise to trust Jesus on this one.

Still, Jesus doesn't say that the answer is simply to have nothing to do with money or wealth. Not only would that be difficult, if not impossible, but Jesus never seemed to be about a world-denying or ascetic faith. He enjoyed a good meal and good wine. He seemed to notice the beauty of nature. He didn't mind someone throwing a party or even splurging and being a little extravagant, as in the case of the woman who anointed his feet. So the answer to the question of money is not trying to run away from it, figuratively "burying" it (see Matt. 25:14ff.).

The real question is what's first in your life? After warning his disciples that "you cannot serve God and wealth," he went on to speak, famously, of the birds of the air that neither sow nor reap and the lilies of the field that neither toil nor spin. He is not telling us to pretend that we are birds or flowers. He is saying that some things are first in order of importance, namely, God and God's way and realm, and some things are not first and not to be put into first position in our lives. When we put things that are secondary in the first spot, life eventually gets screwed up. When we "major in the minors" things get all out of whack.

It's this way in the church too. We sometimes put secondary things, like more members in the first spot or make it the most important thing. That almost never works. We have to put good, faithful, and bold ministry in God's name first, and membership growth tends to follow.

Here Jesus tells us to put first things first. "Strive for the Kingdom of God and his righteousness, and all these things will be given to you as well." For some people this seems to be a once-in-a-lifetime decision. For many of us it is a decision that needs to be made and re-affirmed over and over again, sometimes every day. Unlike the birds and flowers, we are human beings who have the capacity for choice and for commitment. Jesus challenges us, in love if not gentleness, to be clear and intentional about who we are, about whose we are, and what we're about. Such a challenge seems to me a gift.

Takeaways

1. Money is not neutral. While it certainly can be used in good and faithful ways, it has a seductive power. We human beings can and do make an idol of money. (A friend once defined an idol as "anything you can't laugh at." Think how often, when money is at issue, someone says, "This is no laughing matter," or we are *deadly* serious.) Reflect on a time that you have seen the power of money have an ill effect on people and relationships. Think of a time when you have seen money used well and in service to God.

2. Jesus reminds us that we, as human beings, have both power and responsibility. We have the power, at least in some measure, to determine what's first or most important in our lives. And we are responsible, in some measure, for our choices and for the lives we lead and the people we become. (I say "in some measure" because neither our power nor our responsibility are absolute or unconditioned). Struggle with this question, "What is first in my life?" Seek God's guidance and grace in moving your actions and choices to align more nearly with your core values. Be prepared to ask forgiveness too.

John 2:1–12, Better Than You Ever Imagined

This is the story of the wedding at Cana, when Jesus performed his first "sign." John prefers the word "sign" to "miracle," although they mean much the same. A sign points beyond itself. It points to God.

So here the wine ran out. Jesus had a testy little exchange with his mother, but then gave the word. He pointed to the six giant stone jars that were there at the wedding so the guests might purify themselves when the party was over. Jesus directed the servants to fill the jars to the brim, then to draw some out and take it to the steward of the wedding feast. When they did, the steward exclaimed, "Everyone serves the good wine first, and then the inferior wine after the guests have become drunk. But you have kept the good wine until now."

The steward, and most of the guests, saw only the wine. Some few got that this was a sign. They saw beyond the wine itself. They saw God's glory in Jesus.

But here's the really telling detail. Jesus replaced water with wine. He replaced purity with power. In the place of religious ritual, Jesus offered God's real presence. Moreover, note the quantities involved. Six stone jars, each holding twenty or thirty gallons. It's not as if Jesus came up with a few extra bottles of wine, or even a case or two. Suddenly they were awash in wine, the finest wine, the equivalent of over 750 bottles of it. What's up with that?

Part of what's up with it is that Jesus is inviting people beyond religion as going through the rituals to faith as encounter with the living God. And like almost all the signs in John, what people discover is this: when Jesus is present and at work what results is far more than they expected would happen or ever imagined was possible. Jesus doesn't just meet our expectations, he goes far beyond them. Sometimes in other experiences in life something similar happens. We expected one thing but it turned out to be so much more than we expected. "We knew we were having a baby, but we never imagined how amazing it would be." "Yes, I was looking for a church, but I never expected this, a community and experience that have changed my life." "We went on a trip together, a vacation, but it became so much more than that."

Takeaways

1. Generous giving is sometimes inspired by having our eyes opened to just how full, how blessed, how overflowing life really is. There is a sense of an abundance or grace that goes far beyond what we imagined or expected. Can you recall times in your life when you have experienced something like this? What was going on? How did it affect you and the way you lived after?

2. In an effort to deepen our own sense of the abundance of life, particularly in our church, ponder for a few moments all the places in the life of your congregation where you sense God's presence. Name those and share them with one another. Compare this focus on where you sense God's presence in your church with our frequent focus on our problems or failings in the church. How does each focus affect you or your group?

Acts 4:32–5:11

This passage begins with a snapshot of the early church. "Now the whole group of those who believed were of one heart and soul, and no one claimed private ownership of any possessions, but everything they owned they held in common." These few words tend to elicit strong reactions. Some people recoil, put off by what they see as an early expression of communism or communalism. The idea that no one has "private property" is to some deeply troubling. Others react to this snapshot of the early church quite differently, perhaps wistfully. They may say something like, "I wish our church could be like that, truly united, truly sharing, but that will never happen."

However you react to this description of life in the early church, one thing is very evident. In Acts money and how it is used have everything to do with the life of faith and the experience of Christ and his resurrection power. We cannot read this passage or the whole Book of Acts and put money and faith in different compartments. Overall, the perspective of Acts is that how we use money is an accurate barometer of our spiritual condition.

That leads to the next disturbing part of this passage. Acts author Luke gives us two contrasting examples of the use of wealth and its consequences. One, the story of Barnabas (4:36–37), is a positive example; the other, the story of Ananias and Sapphira (5:1–11), is negative.

In the first we meet Barnabas, who is a Jewish priest, a Levite. Though priests weren't supposed to own land, Barnabas evidently did. But he sold his land and brought the money to lay at the feet of the apostles so that they might use it to see that there was "not a needy person among them" (4:34). If land ownership had been a little sketchy for priest Barnabas, his heart had been transformed by grace and overflowed in generosity. Somewhat like the case of Zacchaeus the tax collector (see Luke 19), Barnabas's generosity is a sign of his new life and redemption.

Next up is Ananias, who claims to have done something similar to what Barnabas had done, that is, sell a property and bring the proceeds to the apostles to help those in need. That's what Ananias claimed he had done. It's not what he did. He claimed to be generous, but he wasn't. While claiming to give all, what he did was keep part of the proceeds for himself and lied about it. The problem here is less greed than it is deception. Peter confronted Ananias, who upon hearing the truth spoken out loud and before everyone, dropped dead on the spot. That can happen when the image you present to others is exposed as a false one. You die. (Note: neither God nor Peter "killed" him. He dropped dead.) Subsequently, Sapphira, the wife of Ananias, arrived. When it became clear that she was in on the deception, Peter confronted her as well, and she too dropped dead. They were allied in presenting a phony picture of themselves to others.

Okay, this is a challenging story. It sounds as if God or the apostles have punished Ananias and Sapphira. But we're not actually told that. We are only told that when their deceit and false self was exposed they fell over dead. It is probably not wise for congregations or their leaders to say that something similar will happen to people who don't fulfill their pledge! But what may be wise for leaders to say is that how we use money is a matter of life and death. And it may be wise to suggest that every time we hoard money we die a little bit. And when hoarding becomes our way of life, we may find that we are dead, spiritually. We might also say that pretending to be one thing when we are really something different is a real killer, especially when the truth is revealed. And on the other hand, in Barnabas we see extraordinary acts of generosity that provide encouragement to many others. In fact, the name "Barnabas" means "one who encourages" or "son of encouragement."

Takeaways

1. "How we use money is a matter of life and death." What do you think? Is that true? When and how have you seen the truth of that statement?

2. In Acts the way that people use money provides an accurate barometer of their spiritual condition. If that is the case, what would you say is the barometric reading for your church? Are you in a spiritually healthy place? Or do you seem to have some heart disease or occlusion of the arteries? Is there even some tendency to say one thing, as Ananias and Sapphira did, but do something altogether different?

3. We can provide encouragement to others with our positive examples of faith and generosity, as did Barnabas. Who has been a Barnabas, a person of encouragement, when it comes to the practice of stewardship or generosity for you?

A Closing Theological Postscript

In concluding I want to offer a theological insight that is core to our faith. I want to do so by considering the offering as a part of worship.

There was a time when the offering was one of the "preliminaries" before the sermon, which ended the service. Worship renewal and reform has restored the offering to a point in the service similar to worship in the early church. Now the offering is later in the service, given in response to hearing a word from the Lord and the gospel message of good news. In this respect, the offering helps us to understand something basic to the Christian way of life.

Ours is a life lived in response, in response to God's grace and mercy. That comes first. God's doing comes first. Our doing, offering of money, prayers, our lives, is in response to God's grace. The Protestant Reformers put this in terms of a helpful aphorism. "Salvation is all about grace; ethics is all about gratitude." Salvation is God's work or grace. The grace invites and expects a response on our part, which is a loving and holy life, lived in grateful response.

Sometimes we get this wrong. We imagine that our efforts, projects, or good deeds, will cause God to love us or win God to our side. When that becomes our basic assumption, the result is feverish and frustrating activity, anger at God, and resentment toward others. Grace comes first. We don't have to win God's love, God gives it freely. We don't have to try to get on God's good side. In Christ, God takes our side.

So the offering in worship, the humble offering, is at the heart of our way of life. We respond in gratitude, not just in worship, but in all of life. Our lives are our response to a loving and gracious God, who has taken our side and will never leave it. Week by week, we are reminded of and grow in this way of life, a life lived in grateful response to a gracious God. We might call that "Stewardship."

Five

Leadership, Trust, and Creating a Culture of Giving

In this chapter I want to focus on the role of leadership and on strategies for congregational leaders. In the category of "congregational leadership" I am including pastoral leadership, a congregation's staff, the governing boards, and the team or committee that is leading the stewardship ministry or program.

The leadership strategies that I discuss here are ones that apply to the overall life and leadership of a congregation. Moreover, they are the seven strategies that are the core of the first book in this Congregational Vitality series, my *Leadership for Vital Congregations*. Here I will briefly describe each strategy in a general way and then adapt it particularly for leadership in the area of stewardship. In a sense, I am asking readers to exercise a bifocal vision as I discuss leadership strategies. Through the distance lens, I want you to be thinking of congregational leadership in a larger and more general way. Through the near vision lens I will be applying each strategy to stewardship in particular.

This approach builds on a central argument of this book as a whole, which is that stewardship cannot be considered in isolation from the overall life, health, and vitality of the congregation. Many of our congregations, and their leaders, are facing questions of overall church vitality and direction. Stewardship has to be considered in this context. Michael Durall reminds us, "Stewardship is not separate from the ongoing life of the congregation; it mirrors congregational life as a whole. For example, if people come to church out of routine or habit and have low expectations of what the church can accomplish or how their lives will be changed, then stewardship initiatives will reflect these attitudes." Durall is right when he says (and which I noted earlier), "You cannot take a congregation that is somnolent for 11 months of the year and make the members wildly enthusiastic about giving during the 12th."[1]

There is, as the saying goes, both bad news and good news here. The bad news is that if the patient is in generally bad health, even dying, then replacing one part alone won't make a big difference. But there's good news too. Often stewardship can be a catalyst for wider transformation as it may provoke us to face questions that are at the heart of congregational vitality. These are questions, suggested earlier, of our central purpose or mission. Why are we here? Why has God called us to be here? What are we trying to accomplish? Not only can the particular area of stewardship raise these questions, which are a wonderful entry point to congregational renewal and redirection, but stewardship also has a great potential for impacting the lives of individuals and families, challenging and deepening their faith.

The larger issue here is our stewardship of the church of Jesus Christ. Paul spoke of ministers as "stewards of the mysteries of God." All of us are stewards of the gift of God called "church." Good stewardship is manifested (or not) in a host of related ways, one of which is our financial support of the church's life and ministries. Shall we be found to have been faithful in our stewardship of the church of Jesus Christ?

Strategy Number One: Building Trust

Trust is the currency of leadership. It is also something like the red blood cells or immune system of a congregation. Without trust, it's tough to make much headway as a leader. And when trust is absent or diminished in the life of a congregation, it is particularly vulnerable to infections and illness.

How is trust built? Slowly. It takes time. And it takes being intentional. In *Leadership for Vital Congregations*, I broke the work of building trust into three components: character, relationship, and competence.

What is "character" or good character? In the Book of Acts when the apostles asked the community to select from among themselves the seven

48

people who would be the church's first deacons, they said that these should be people "of good standing, full of the Spirit and of wisdom" (Acts 6:3). That's not a bad definition of character. It includes a person's public estimation, spiritual depth or maturity, and practical wisdom. In *Leadership for Vital Congregations*, I wrote that "character" means that "your words have to match your deeds; that you listen if not more than, then at least as well as you speak. It means that when you promise to do something, you get it done."[2] Character means that you are a person of integrity. That doesn't mean that you are perfect. We all make mistakes and depend on God's grace and the forgiveness of others. Perhaps an awareness of our fallibility and imperfection is also part of a good or strong character.

The other components of building trust are relationships and competence. Good leaders make a point of building relationships. For pastors this means that you don't spend all your time in your office or study, but that you get out into the life of the congregation and community. You visit people in their homes and places of work. When people are going through a hard time, you connect with them. For lay leaders in a congregation this means that you take time for people that you are leading or working with to get to know each other as people. Maybe you have everyone on your team over for dinner or a picnic without an agenda. You take time to visit with people at the coffee hour and help out on the projects of others in the church.

We also build trust by being competent. This doesn't mean that a preacher has to hit a home run every week in her sermon, but that she does prepare and preach a coherent and reasonably inspiring message. It means that you are a sensitive presence and listener during times of crisis. And it means that you help a congregation to identify its real and important challenges and to make progress on those. For lay leaders competence includes the capacity to put together a focused agenda, to keep a meeting on track, to think through tough challenges, and to participate in opportunities to sharpen your skills.

The significance of trust and building trust for stewardship is enormous. *In many ways, giving is tied to relationship.* This goes in both directions. If people in the congregation feel known and cared about, they are much more likely to give generously. And, in the other direction, if people know you, a pastor or lay leader, and feel that they have a relationship with you and trust you, again they are much more likely to give generously in support of the church and its ministry. This doesn't mean developing relationships simply in order to get people to give. People see through that. But it does mean that you take the time and make the effort to get to know people and build relationships. You find out who people are, what they care about, and what people and experiences have impacted their lives. Pastors have a great opportunity here in the practice of pastoral calling. Alas, too many clergy have given this up. I understand that pastoral calling isn't as easy today with people's lives being busy and fragmented. But it is possible. And sometimes a pastoral call can be made over the phone, too.

Another implication of the leadership strategy of building trust when it comes to stewardship is that opportunities need to be created where church leaders ask people what they are thinking and in particular what they are thinking about the church and about their financial support. Six months before a stewardship program or canvass, simply invite a group of key people, meaning people (as in Acts) of good standing, spiritual depth, and wisdom, to get together. Ask them how they think things are going. What are our church's strengths? Needs? Explore why they give to the church and to other charitable causes or institutions. What motivates their giving? It may be that a pastor can have this kind of conversation with people. Or it may work better if it's a trusted lay leader facilitating the conversation. In some instances it may be useful to have a wise "outsider" facilitate the conversation, assuring people that what they say will not be attributed by name though the general sense of the meeting and insights gleaned will be helpful to the church's leadership and in planning for the future. The same kinds of conversations can also be undertaken on a one-to-one basis. Often leaders assume that they know where people are at or what motivates their giving. This may not be true.

Strategy Number Two: Defining Reality

Sometimes leaders imagine that being a leader means they know what to do or what needs to be done. That can be a dangerous assumption. Wise leaders begin with questions, not answers. They start by asking, "What's going on here?" "What is the character or 'genius' of this congregation?" "What is this congregation's story?" "What opportunities exist for this congregation now?" "What's going on in the town, city, or community in which the congregation is set?" "What is God doing here?"

As leaders build trust through good character, developing relationships, and exercising and exhibiting competence, leaders are also trying to figure out what is going on and to define reality. Ron Heifetz, who teaches leaders and leadership, has a phrase for this. He calls it "Getting to the balcony."[3] Leaders need to get up above the dance floor of congregational life to get a better look and to see the patterns of interaction.

In the area of stewardship figuring out what's going on and defining reality is critically important and sometimes very challenging. It includes figuring out what the actual giving patterns are and what the potential is.

I recall my first stewardship program and capital drive at my first church. Shortly after we had engaged the person who would be our consultant, he called the committee together and said, "This evening we need to figure out what the potential is here." He had, with the help of the church secretary and treasurer, put the names of each individual or family on a 5 inch x 7 inch card, along with the address and phone number and their current pledge. He announced that we were going to go through the congregation and estimate the annual income of that person or family. I think he had this coded alphabetically so that, for example, AB meant $10 to $15,000 annual income, BC meant $15,000 to $20,000 and so on up. It was the alphabetical code that we wrote on the cards.

As he announced what we were about to do, I admit that I was taken aback, for two reasons. First, all ten or twelve of those present were soon to find out what every person and family in the congregation currently gave. Second, the assumption was that this group had a pretty accurate idea about the income of everyone in the congregation. Could that be true, I wondered?

So here we bump right away into what is an important challenge: secrecy. Many congregations have a longstanding practice that what anyone gives should be kept secret, or "confidential," and that no one, except perhaps the financial secretary or treasurer, should have any idea of this information. While I believe that such information should be treated with respect and care, secrecy is a mistake—for a couple of reasons. Almost anything that is treated as a deep, dark secret tends to accumulate undue and often unhealthy power. The truth is, as noted in the previous chapter, money can and does become an idol, one that exercises enormous and unhealthy power. We unmask and disempower idols (false gods) by exposing them. This means talking about money openly and honestly. It is part of why I, as a pastor, have occasionally been quite open with a congregation about my own stewardship and giving.

Another reason that secrecy is a mistake is simple: it undermines a congregation's stewardship and their capacity to grow in generosity. Based on wide experience Michael Durall concludes, "I have found that the higher the level of secrecy, the lower the level of giving."[4] Another way to put this is to say that secrecy makes the creation of a culture of giving all but impossible. We are influenced by the example and faith of others. If that is all secret or treated as if it were, then we are severely handicapped.

One aspect of this is the pastor's knowledge of what members pledge or give. I've encountered ministers who declare with some evident pride that "I have no idea what people give, nor do I wish to know." Their pride seems to owe to an assumption that somehow money is impure or bad and that their concerns are of a higher nature or "more spiritual." This is a completely un-biblical and un-Christian separation of the "material" and "spiritual." Christianity is a rather material faith. The Son of God was "made flesh," after all, and "dwelt among us full of truth and grace" (John 1:14). When Jesus told his disciples how to know his presence, he took a loaf of bread and a cup of wine and said, "Eat this, drink this." All very earthy and material. Part of the reason we include an offering in our worship is to build a bridge between our daily (Monday to Friday) lives and our Sunday worship.

Sometimes clergy allege that knowing what people give may effect how they treat people, meaning that they will favor some because they give a lot or disregard others because they give little. If that's true they probably shouldn't be ministers in the first place! I would argue the opposite. Being aware of people's giving pattern provides important information to a pastor. If people's pledge or giving goes south, that may be an indication of something going on in their life and family, or in their relationship with God or the church. On the other hand, if giving jumps or rises gradually that too means something. Moreover, I have thought it important to be able to acknowledge and thank people for their gifts and generosity.

I know that someone will point to the Scripture in which Jesus says, "Whenever you give alms, do not sound a trumpet before you [and] do not let your left hand know what your right hand is doing" (Matt. 6:2–3). Yes, we should guard against grandstanding or boasting. But Jesus also said, "Let your light shine before others, so that they may see your good works and give glory to your Father in heaven" (Matt.5:16). I think philosopher Peter Singer is right when he urges in his book on ending world poverty that we need to "Get It [Giving] Into the Open." We tend, Singer argues, "To do what others in our 'reference group'—those with whom we identify—are doing."[5] We really are encouraged, instructed, and inspired by the example of the generosity of others. Rather than creating cultures of secrecy, with its companion, fear, churches ought to be aiming to create cultures of giving and generosity.

Back, then, to that night when our fund drive consultant took out his cards with information about people's current giving and said that we would now go through the entire congregation person by person or family by family to estimate what their annual income was and thus determine our "giving potential." I thought, "Surely, we don't know that about everyone." Wrong. It turned out that between the dozen or so people in the room we had a pretty good idea of what everyone in the congregation was making to within a couple of thousand dollars. So much for secrecy! When the meeting was over that night we knew two things: how much we, as a congregation and members of it, currently gave in support of God's work through the church, and a pretty good idea of what people, again the congregation as a whole and members of it, had to work with it and our potential.

We discovered that as a congregation our giving level or percentage of income was currently at about 1.5 percent. In that we were pretty much on track with most mainline Protestant congregations where the giving level tends to average about 1.7 percent (contrast this to the Assembly of God denomination, the fastest growing in North America, where the giving level is 11 percent, or to the Mormons, as some other denominations, where 10 percent is the norm and pattern). Our consultant reiterated his proposal that we put before the congregation a goal, a "challenge pledge goal," of 5 percent total giving to God's work through the church. Since we were doing a capital drive, we would ask people to divide their 5 percent between two budgets, one for the operating budget and the other for the capital budget.

Strategy number two is "defining reality." That evening we took some giant steps in that direction. Often it can be helpful to a congregation, especially one that has fallen into the secrecy/fear trap, to have an outside consultant be involved and to be focusing on a capital drive. The outside "expert" is able to challenge people in ways that insiders may not be able to do. And the occasion of a capital drive creates a sense of urgency and challenge that a "regular" annual program may not. This doesn't mean that you cook up a capital project where none exists. It does mean that if there's a need now or in the near future for a capital drive it may represent a real opportunity.

Strategy Number Three: Why Are We Here?

This third leadership strategy reprises the core theme of chapter 2, a congregation's purpose or mission. There's no need to repeat all that I said there. I would simply underscore the importance of being able to talk honestly and convincingly about why we are here as a congregation. What do we see as the reason God has called us to exist? What is it that God has called us to do? Whose lives do we seek to touch and change and how do we propose to do that? Or to recall the words of that New England pastor, "What is our overarching purpose?"

Another way to approach these core questions is to recall the questions that the well-known consultant Peter Drucker made famous. Drucker was known for asking two questions of his clients, "What business are you in?" and "How's business?" Of course, the church is not a business in the sense of a profit-making business. Nevertheless, we ought to ask and be able to answer these questions in our context and for our congregation. What is our "business"?

When we adapt and apply this to stewardship it means two things. First, it means that we are able to describe succinctly and with clarity the mission or purpose of the church (again, for examples of church purpose or mission statements, see Appendix Two). Second, it means that we offer people a goal for their giving. Let's go back to that meeting where we went through the 5 inch × 7 inch cards and we determined our current giving level and our potential giving level.

We had covered a lot of ground that night, but we weren't done quite yet. Our consultant said there was one more thing we needed to discuss that night. "I need," he said, "to put before you, the leaders of this congregation and of this stewardship ministry a challenge. I need to ask you to accept our challenge pledge goal of giving at least 5 percent of your income to God's work through this church. Because," he continued, "we are doing a capital drive as well as the campaign for the operating budget, you will need to divide your giving between the two, making two pledges. I ask you to prayerfully consider and make a commitment to a total pledge of at least 5 percent. I understand that some of you already give that or more. But what we need to be able to say to the congregation is that we, the leaders of the congregation, have accepted this goal and challenge and that we invite others to join us."

Note what has happened here. A goal has been set and a focus given. So the "Why Are We Here?" question/strategy has been addressed. But we've also addressed strategies one and two. By being able to say, "We, the pastor and leaders of the church, have committed ourselves to this goal," we created trust among ourselves and with the congregation. We were not asking them to do something we had not done ourselves. And, second, we had defined reality. We knew where we stood.

Michael Durall offers the following observation about the role of leaders in this respect. "In many churches, parishioners will not give more than the minister and members of the governing board are giving. Even if parishioners don't know what the minister or board members give, they have an uncanny sixth sense about not being too far out in front of anyone else, especially the leadership."[6]

Strategy Number Four: Write the Vision

I distinguish "purpose" and "vision" in the following way: "purpose" is our reason for being, what God has called us to do; "vision" means our near-term (five years) priorities based on our purpose. So if our purpose is "to grow people of faith who participate in God's work in the world," our vision might be made up of three to five priorities that will help us to more faithfully and fruitfully fulfill our core mission or purpose.

In the best of all possible worlds, a congregation does have both a purpose statement and a vision, that is, a focused list of key priorities for this chapter in the congregation's life. If you do have those, then during the stewardship drive is a great time to repeat, reinforce, and reinterpret both your purpose and your vision. If you don't have those, refer back to chapter 2 for how to proceed to put them in place.

An alternative way to proceed that often is part of stewardship at this point is to utilize a congregation's proposed budget. I know some congregations that develop a detailed budget before their stewardship campaign, and their "vision" is based and reflected in the budget. That's fine, so long as the priorities are not lost in the detail of line items and accounts. I know other congregations that do not develop their budget until the stewardship program is over and they know how much they have to work with. In such cases the stewardship program is conducted on the basis of existing purpose/mission and vision/priorities statements. That's okay too. I don't know that either one is right. It probably has a lot to do with the culture of your particular congregation.

It is fine to refer to a proposed budget, so long as we also have (or are working to get) a sense and statement of purpose/mission as well as major priorities or vision. I see a budget as a resource here, but not as a primary focus. When too much emphasis is placed on the budget and on particular line item details, it tends to distract from the more important dual foci of our overarching purpose as a church and stewardship as a spiritual practice. So have a budget available if that's your pattern or style, but don't base your giving goals (as with our first Mr. Jones) on the budget or the percent the budget has gone up this year.

In terms of a package of available resources for those who wish them, the budget should be paired with a current financial statement and an auditor's report. (Note: I recommend having these available, not automatically distributing them to everyone, with the risk that people get lost in the details.) The point here is that people have a right to expect that the money they give will be soundly managed. Instances of financial malfeasance in churches continue to be reported. When this happens the effects are serious and long-lasting. Smaller congregations must avoid the situation where only one person is looking at the books. Most mid-size and large congregations need to shell out for a professional audit every couple of years.

Strategy Number Five: Managing Distress

When leaders ask people to change, to reevaluate commitments and values and to alter habits and behaviors, it is likely, if not certain, that there will be some level of resistance. Some "distress" will be introduced into the system or life of a congregation. While that is not an easy or pleasant thing to experience, it's not a bad thing to have happen. Resistance is a sign that something important is at stake. The trick is to have enough distress going on that people are motivated but not so much that they balk or shut down. One of the tasks of leadership and leaders in a church is to gauge and evaluate the level of distress and to try to keep it in a workable and productive range. It's pretty much the same challenge that a teacher or a coach faces. You have to figure out how to balance encouragement with challenge, acceptance with expectation. While there is no formula for this, if leaders are aware that gauging this and working toward a productive balance is part of their job, that's an important start. Having and using purpose and a vision helps to keep resistance to manageable levels. That is, if there is a sense of direction, resistance is reduced.

Some expressions of distress that churches experience in relation to stewardship are predictable. "All this church wants is our money." Or, "There's too much talk about money around here these days." Or, "I think it's just awful that people are talking to the congregation about how much they pledge—whoever heard of such a thing!" Another popular and predictable way of venting steam is "poor talk." "You know pastor, you come from a wealthy community, but people around here aren't like that. People here are just scraping by." Or, sometimes we veil self-interest behind concern for others, "You know lots of people in this congregation are on fixed incomes."

There's a good chance that all of these things will be said or heard, and probably a few more I haven't thought of. Take it in stride. Stay on your goals. Tell yourself that some pushback is a sign that you're onto something important, because it is! Monitor the level of distress and figure out ways to moderate or lower it if it threatens to blow up.

Much of what I've described in the previous strategies and chapters are ways to "turn up" the level of distress so that people are challenged. What are some ways to turn down or moderate the level of distress if it seems to be getting too hot?

Here are some suggestions for lowering the temperature:

1. Provide good information and within reason provide it to everyone. Avoid knowledge in-groups or some who get to be in the know and others who aren't.

2. Keep the people connections strong. Make your pastoral visits. Show up in the hospital. If you are a lay leader, take time to visit with people at the coffee hour. Consider having some events that have been popular or "golden oldies" in the past, so that alongside the new challenges there are some familiar activities and experiences.

3. Utilize key and respected lay leaders as sources of information, assurance, and example. Be sure that some of the people in the congregation who are "of good standing, spiritual depth, and wisdom" are given ways to say that they support this and why.

4. Return to the purpose and vision, keeping the core message about mission in front of people. A clear sense of direction moderates distress.

5. Be in touch with and manage your own anxiety as a leader. If you find yourself being short with someone or popping off at another, step back and get a grip. Communicate your belief in the mission and goals, but don't get too anxious about the outcomes or overidentified personally with the project.

6. Let people know that you've done your homework and that you have made use of appropriate specialists or experts, whether in construction or

program development or fundraising. Needless to say, this should be real and solid, not smoke and mirrors.

Strategy Number Six: Persistence

Change happens slowly, but it does happen. Often leaders give up too soon, or they expect change or even wholesale transformation to happen over night. We live in a "quick fix" culture. Especially if a congregation has been in existence for many years, change takes time. Therefore, leaders must be prepared to be persistent.

If this is true of leadership and change generally, it is particularly true in the stewardship area. If you are making shifts like some of those we have discussed and described, for example, from a culture of secrecy to a culture of getting it in the open, that's big. It will take time. If you're making a shift from a congregation that was more or less asleep and simply maintaining or slowly declining to one that is animated by a sense and statement of purpose and mission, that's big. It will take time. If you are making a move from patterns of giving where there were no particular goals other than "the budget has gone up 3 percent this year, folks" to the modern tithe (5 percent) that's big. It will take time. All of these are shifts in the culture of a congregation. In my experience you are talking about a five-year piece of work with such shifts.

Often in the stewardship area we imagine that doing things different for one year will result in complete and lasting change. Forget that. Congregations have a tremendous capacity to settle back into what they have long known and been comfortable with. You should be prepared to work at stewardship over a longer term and to develop a practice that is sustainable. If you do find a good consultant, consider engaging that person not just for one pull-out-all-the-stops year or drive, but for a period of three to five years. And be prepared to bring new people onto the leadership team so that the learning and change gets spread more deeply and broadly throughout the congregation.

Strategy Number Seven: Become a Learning Organization

As you work at any important challenges in the life of the congregation you will learn things. Some things you try will work well, others will not. Some that you try one year you will discover ways to improve in the future. Most importantly, if you set some goals and then follow through, do assessments along the way, and if you come to a conclusion or end point, ponder and share what you've learned.

58

In working with some larger congregations I suggest using a strategic planning approach, developing five-year plans, which included the purpose and vision components I described earlier. The first time through it is tough. People aren't quite sure what we are doing or whether it will prove worthwhile. The second time around is easier because we have learned from the first time. We were functioning as a learning organization. By the third time we did this work people thought, "This is what we have always done," because they had learned a new set of skills and the culture of the congregation had changed. But note: that was over a ten-year time span.

In the stewardship area paying attention to data collected, to skills learned, and to insights gained will prove to be worth a great deal. It will be good information and learning for future leaders of that congregation, and some of what is learned will be the kind of thing that can be generalized to other situations and shared with other congregations, as I have been doing here.

In this chapter we have looked at seven leadership strategies. In each instance I have invited you to exercise bi-focal vision, seeing how these strategies apply broadly in the life of the church as well as in the particular arena of stewardship.

Questions for Reflection, Discussion, and Action

1. What particular themes or insights or ideas "jumped out at you" in this chapter?

2. How would you describe or evaluate the trust quotient in your congregation? High, low, or somewhere in between? What has contributed to trust? What has damaged or diminished it? What needs to be done to build trust now?

3. How did you respond to the discussion in this chapter of secrecy in the church with regard to money and giving? Do you think that "Getting It [Giving, Generosity, Stewardship] into the Open" is a valuable idea? Why or why not? What steps need to be taken in your congregation for "Getting It into the Open" and creating a culture of giving?

Six

Tony's Ten Commandments

The last two chapters have been on the longer side. You deserve a reward for working through those long chapters. This chapter is short. Inspiration for this chapter comes from my friend and colleague Mike Bennett, a United Church of Christ minister in Massachusetts. Mike was supposed to write this book, but he copped out. So I don't feel too bad about "stealing" his ideas (he gave me permission).

These "Ten Commandments for Pastoral Leadership in Stewardship" will reinforce some points I've already touched on. While this list is directed, first of all, to pastors, it has implications for everyone who is involved in giving leadership on stewardship in a congregation.

First Commandment: Thou Shalt Live It

It's simple really. You can't ask people to do what you don't do yourself. This doesn't mean constantly dwelling on your own giving. Still less does it mean boasting. It's a matter of integrity. Walking the talk. Nor does this mean that you don't find it a struggle at times to practice what you preach. It's okay that you find it a challenge, even a struggle at times. You can acknowledge that.

Second Commandment: Thou Shalt Talk About It

Just to be clear, the "it" is stewardship, the relationship between faith and money, generosity and stewardship as spiritual practices. Probably there are two extremes to be avoided: talking about it too much and talking about it too little. But it's important to demythologize the sacred taboo of money by talking about it openly and honestly. Do use your own story and witness, as I have in this book, but do so sparingly and strategically.

Stewardship should be talked about with new members and in new member orientation groups or classes. Often newer members are among the most enthusiastic about the church. Moreover, newer members often wish to know what's expected. Goals can and should be presented as guidelines with the encouragement to work toward them in ways that work for you.

Third Commandment: Thou Shalt Help People Talk About It

Find safe ways to talk about money and its role in our lives. Scripture is an ally. Jesus is too. Both bring the subject up fairly often. Try to talk about money in our lives when it's not "stewardship time." Talk also about the larger themes of growing in faith, a faith that is real and makes a difference in our lives and the lives of others. Share stories of people who have found joy and meaning in being generous givers. During stewardship time encourage people to think and talk about money without focusing only on the church's goals, but also on their experience, struggles, questions about money and their faith and fears.

Many churches have something like "stewardship moments" at worship during the stewardship campaign. There are a lot of ways to go about this. You can ask people to talk about how they've experienced God's presence in their lives and in the life and ministry of the church in the last year. You can also ask people to talk about their own pledging, giving, what they will be doing and how they've arrived at that decision or commitment. Again, this is part of "Getting It into the Open," creating a culture of giving, and disempowering fear/empowering faith. You can have someone tell the story of another person's giving and how it has impacted his or her life.

Fourth Commandment: Thou Shalt Get Specific

It's helpful to use real numbers and not vague generalities. Often people don't have a clear idea of what's expected or asked. Often they want that, to know what we're asking or expecting. Avoid, as I've indicated, giving goals that are tied to percentage increases in the budget (the first Mr. Jones). Avoid asking everyone to do the same thing. "Let's all give $100 more this year." Do consider using proportionate giving, encouraging people to give a percentage of their total income. Provide information about what that means in real dollars at different income levels. It's often helpful to provide a table of current pledges, meaning so many pledges under $500, this many between $500 and $1000 and so on up, including, "This many between $5000 and $6000, this many over $10,000. Remember people tend to do what those in their "reference group," those with whom we identify, are doing.

Fifth Commandment: Thou Shalt Ask and Equip Others to Ask

You'd be surprised how often when people are asked why they give money to support this or that they will say, "Well, I believe in it *and* I was asked." You'd also be surprised, or maybe not, how often people in the church say, "I could give more, but no one ever asked me to." While some people (see chapter 10) will say, "I'll do anything but ask for money," others enjoy doing so and see inviting people to give to something worthwhile as an opportunity both for themselves and the person they ask. After all, you're not asking for the money for yourself. You're asking for the ministry and witness of the church of Jesus Christ.

Sixth Commandment: Thou Shalt Not Sweat the Zeros and Near Zero

By "zeros" I mean those who make no pledge and in effect don't give at all. Committees love to focus on the zeros. Don't let them. Leave them to God's grace. Focus on those engaged, who are growing, who are with the program. It's an old teacher's technique, which is, you give your attention and praise to the students who are doing what you want them to do instead of giving attention to and thus reenforcing negative behaviors.

Seventh Commandment: Thou Shalt Make the Stewardship Committee Look at the List of Pledges

Again, we're against secrecy and for getting it into the open as a general principle. Beyond that people in the church often have unrealistic ideas about where the money comes from (they may think it magically appears). Do have people on the stewardship committee who are "of good standing, spiritually mature, and wise," and who will not use their knowledge in unfair, unwise, or foolish ways. You do need to have a group of people and leaders in the church who get real.

Eighth Commandment: Thou Shalt Debunk "Poor Talk"

It's sometimes amazing how poor or strapped people suddenly become around stewardship time. It's amazing that people who have money for a new car in March are really hurting in November. It's odd that people are able to take expensive vacations in June but are barely getting by in October. The point is not that people shouldn't buy a new car or take a vacation. The point is that most mainline Protestant congregations are made up of middle- and upper-middle class people, not poor people. Sure, there are exceptions, but poor talk is often just that, talk.

In one congregation I served, a congregation that was mostly middle- or upper-middle class, the stewardship committee chair did her homework. She said that if we're currently giving at 5 percent that would mean that about half the congregation are below the officially established U.S. poverty level. "We know that's not true, don't we?" she said. She continued, "It would also mean that the next 40 percent of the congregation have an income of $60,000 or less. Well, we know that's not the case, is it?"

Poor talk often stems from and encourages a scarcity mentality. Better to encourage a spirit and attitude of abundance. As Michael Durall puts it, "Giving is the nature of God. In giving to the church, we give to strengthen our own congregation, to help the less fortunate, and to deepen our relationship with God. Churches should not take an apologetic attitude . . . but should encourage generosity."[1]

Ninth Commandment: Thou Shalt Remember "It's Not the Economy, Stupid"

The issue is the faithfulness of the church, not the U.S. economy. Okay, the economy is there. It's a factor. But not the real factor. When the economy and market were growing rapidly throughout the 1990s charitable giving did not rise; it actually declined as a percent of income. So though a generally good economy may be a factor, it isn't "the economy stupid" after all.

Tenth Commandment: Thou Shalt Value and Take Seriously the Offering as an Act of Worship and Give Some Thought to the Prayer of Dedication

Sometimes the act of offering is trivialized or marginalized in worship. Sometimes worship leaders seem either embarrassed or bothered by it. It is an act of worship. It is offering our selves and our gifts to the one God, the source from "whom all blessings flow." It can and should be a serious and joyful, even a dramatic moment in worship. Sometimes have, as in the early church, a joyful offertory procession where people carry forward their gifts of money, food for the food bank, clothing or blankets for the poor, and bread for communion. Have the choir sing a wonderful anthem as you do. Make the prayer that dedicates the gifts to God real, heartfelt and theologically sound. This is our response to God's graciousness to us. This is our dedication and rededication of ourselves to God. This is building a bridge between our daily lives and Sunday.

So there they are, Tony's (and Mike's) Ten Commandments for Pastoral Leadership/Church Leadership in Stewardship." What do you think?

Questions for Reflection, Discussion, and Action

1. Was there one particular commandment to which you said, murmured or felt an "Amen"?

2. Was there one particular commandment for which you gasped or reached for additional air and thought, "I don't think so"?

3. One church elder (a lay person) said, "If ministers aren't involved in financial matters, it sends a message that money is not an appropriate subject to address in church. It can also be interpreted as the minister abdicating responsibility for a vital part of church life, leaving it to others to deal with."[2] How do you respond to the observation of this church leader?

Seven

Methods and Options for Your Stewardship Ministry

This chapter and the next, "Putting It All Together," are the how-to chapters of this book. My intent in this chapter on "Options" is to describe five different methods or ways of organizing your stewardship drive. I have been a part of each of these five somewhere along the way. For each of the five there will be a basic description of the method, then a section on key steps, and finally an assessment of the strengths and weaknesses of that particular method. Implied in the concluding words of the previous sentence is that there is no one perfect way to do this. Each method has its upsides and its downsides.

Moreover, my experience over thirty years in a variety of different churches and settings is that you do need to change up the method every now and again. When we do the same thing over and over again we lose some spark. So it's a possibility that you will use all five of these at one time or another. One further comment by way of introduction: none of these five are branded, copyrighted stewardship programs. There are many of those out there. The most recent United Church of Christ program is known as *Consecrating Stewards*, for which you can get materials at Local Church Ministries.[1] There are other programs; *Pony Express* is one that some people like.

But it's a little like translations of the Bible. There are now many, many translations of the Bible as well as a host of different "Bibles" for different ages, interests, affinities, or life-stages. While there is something to be said for the diversity of translations and paraphrases, it sometimes seems as if we think, "If only I can find the right translation, then this will be easy." Actually, the Bible is a challenging and difficult book. No translation will take away the challenge or need for hard work on our part. I think it's the same with stewardship. We may think that if we can just find the right program then this will be easy. Sorry. It's work. But it's good work, work worth doing. Through this work you can help your congregation and its members to engage important questions and challenges. You, working with others, can make the difference between a church that is simply getting by and one that is flourishing and a force for the Gospel and for good in the world. And you can change lives by inviting people into a way of life characterized by a giving spirit and a generous heart. If you don't think that those are goals worth working on, then close this book now.

The five methods I want to describe and review are the following:

1. The Every Member Stewardship Canvass (EMSC)
2. Each One Reach One (EORO)
3. Neighborhood-Meeting-Based Stewardship Drive
4. Selective Visitation
5. Mail Only Canvass

Basically, they are in declining order insofar as the effort and the numbers of people and energy involved. They are also in declining order in terms of effectiveness.

Every Member Stewardship Canvass (EMSC)

The intent of this method is see that each member or friend of the church has a face-to-face visit from a trained volunteer who represents the church and the stewardship drive and whose job it is to discuss and receive the pledge of the person or family that they visit.

The organization of the Every Member Stewardship Canvass is intensive and extensive. In addition to the overall planning team or committee, there is the head of the EMSC, then a host of "captains," who each head up a team of "stewardship callers." In addition, there are some auxiliary or support teams, "office," "publicity," and "follow-up."

66

Just how many people are involved depends on the size of the congregation or the number of visits to be made. Generally, you can ask the stewardship callers to do four and five visits in the one- or two-week period of the canvass. I have also seen it done as a one-day canvass in which the callers went out after church and did their four or five calls in one Sunday afternoon or evening. There's a great deal to be said for that one-day format, though you need to ask people to stick around home for the visit or make appointments. And though you may reach a large percentage, there will be some who will be away or who will have to be visited at another time.

The urgency and "let's get it done" sense gained with the one-day visitation tends to diminish as the time allowed for making the visits is extended. I like the one-day approach, with the caveats noted above. Giving a one-week period for the visits to be made is good, two weeks is the longest period practical. Beyond that procrastination tends to take too great a toll and focus is lost.

Here are some of the key steps in the Every Member Stewardship Canvass approach. The first is the choice and calling of the leaders of the EMSC. This should be a person who is enthusiastic about the church and who is strong giver. I also like the idea of co-leaders, with each accepting a two-year commitment. Stagger their terms so one is in his or her first year while the other is in his or her second year. That way you always have one experienced person and one who has fresh eyes.

After the calling of the EMSC leaders, which should be done by the pastor, the board chair, and/or the carry-over leader, the second step is calling the next tier of leaders, the stewardship "captains." They are recruited by the EMSC leader or co-leaders. Again, you want to look for people who are enthusiastic about the church and who are strong givers. Moreover, the strategy with each is to say, "I'm doing this; will you join me?" or "I'm committed to this; will you join me in this commitment?" How many team captains and how many stewardship visitors you need depends on how many calls are to be made.

The next key step in the EMSC format is the training of the stewardship callers. It is crucial to plan a good, effective, tightly structured, inspiring, and informative training session for those who will visit and to insist that everyone attend. At this session you need to be able to talk about the church's purpose or mission, about the vision or priorities, about stewardship as a spiritual practice, about details and logistics of the canvass, the format of the pledge card, and the reporting process. In addition to all this informational content, the training session should include two or more "testimonies" from generous givers about why they do what they do and the meaning of giving for their lives. The training session should include a couple of role play situations (you can have fun with this) where people, especially those who have never done this before, get a chance to see experienced visitors at work or try their hand at it.

The next key step is the visits themselves. Unless you are doing the Sunday one-day intensive and have purposely asked people to stick around home and be ready to receive a caller, the visitor will need to call and make an appointment. Some of those they call will readily make an appointment, but for some it will be difficult to get a time either because they are just busy or because they would rather not have a visit. Visitors need to be prepared for this and stress how important the visit is. They should have been visited themselves already by their team captain, who takes their pledge. So one option is to say, "This is how it works. So-and-so visited me, and now it's my job to visit you, and I'm really looking forward to it." Persistence and politeness are required. Moreover, some people may not be ready to make a pledge on visit number one. Be prepared for that. Be ready to say, "I am more than happy to come back later in the week. When's a good time?" Some people will say, "Just leave the pledge card with me. I'll get it back to you." If you do that, you vastly increase the probability of not getting it back and not getting a pledge at all. The recommended response to this request is, "Sorry, I'm not able to do that. I am responsible to return this card. But I am happy to come again whenever it's convenient for you."

Generally, it's a good idea for a small group of people who really know the church and its members to match the caller with those they will visit. Some people will be better for some visits than others. Generally you want people visiting people who have similar giving potential. And there will be some people who are just oil and water and shouldn't be matched for a visit. Even with prematching you may get some of this and have to redistribute some calls. One more thing, the pledge card should show the pledge amount of the person being visited. This is vital information. But some people will be uncomfortable with that. You'll need to prepare them to receive this information.

In addition to the pledge card, visitors should have a second "Information Card," on which they note any personal information that should be passed on to the pastoral staff or parish care team. For example, "This person has just had surgery," or "There's been a death in family," or "They love/hate the new hymnal," or "They may be interested in making a planned gift," or "They just really need to pray with the pastor or someone." This information should be turned in to the appropriate person on the church board or staff for follow-up. Do follow-up. Sometimes the caller may need to ask, "May I share this [that you've been in the hospital or that you are suffering a spiritual crisis] with the pastor in confidence?"

Basically, the EMSC organization functions as a support and account-ability system with the co-leaders checking in with the captains, the cap-tains checking in with the callers. Some visits will be delightful. Some will be tough. For both its good to check in, touch base, provide encouragement, troubleshoot, and express appreciation. Captains should expect to check in with their team frequently during the period of the drive.

So the key steps are (1) recruitment, (2) training, and (3) the visits them-selves, and (4) follow-up with the visitors for support and accountability.

What are the strengths and weaknesses of the EMSC format? On the strengths side, you will be getting a lot of people involved. The more you have involved and the better the training, the higher the support/giving level. Often 50 percent or more of your total giving will come from those who are volun-teering in the program itself, whether as captains, callers, or backup teams.

In addition to the high level of involvement, you will tend to reach the highest percentage of the congregation with a face-to-face visit with this method. (Do stress the *face-to-face in people's homes* if at all possible. People will try to do something less. "Can't we just touch base at church?" Or "Can't we do this over the phone?" At some point, you may have no choice, but the best is the face-to-face home visit.)

The first time I was a caller in an EMSC format, I had among my calls a family from another country; the dad was a graduate student at the nearby university. I thought, "Wow, this is tough. They have three kids, a tiny apartment, and I'm sure they don't have much money. I don't want to visit them."

But I did. Asi and Rasmina, the father and mother, welcomed me. We talked. We prayed. They made a pledge that exceeded our church's average pledge. They shared how important this was to them and how grateful they were for the church and all that it meant to them, strangers in a strange land, to have a church home. I was deeply moved. That night at the report back I shared this story as others shared other stories of surprise and joy.

For these two reasons the EMSC format is often the best way to go when you're doing a joint drive for a capital fund and operating budget. At such times, congregations typically want to do their best and people tend to be most receptive to a visit as well. It is also likely that at such times a church will hire a fundraising consultant, which does provide a source of norms and an excuse. ("Tom, our fundraising guy, said we have to make face-to-face visits with everyone!") Some churches follow this format every year with good results, but even those that do may need to change it every now and then and try one of the others for a year or two. One advantage of doing it every year is that you will be visiting everyone in the church at least once in a year's time, which is good.

What are the downsides? Pretty much the mirror image of the upsides. An EMSC takes a lot of people and a lot of work. It means recruiting at least one person for every four to five visits. In a larger congregation, that can be over one hundred people. It is also a fairly bold approach, which will result in more contacts and more dollars but will also result in adverse reactions from some. It does require confidence and courage on the part of the callers. In order to minimize unpleasant experiences, you need to do a good up-front job on interpreting your purpose and goals in good publicity, pastoral support, and sharing by people during Sunday services in the weeks before the drive itself. You have to build momentum and enthusiasm to reduce pushback.

Each One Reach One (EORO)

This is a variation on the Every Member Stewardship Canvass. This requires fewer volunteers and fewer visits on the part of any one person but still achieves a personal contact and connection with everyone in the church. Basically, the way it works is this: people are paired. Bill and Susan Brown receive in their mail the pledge card for Dave and Sally Green. Likewise, Dave and Sally receive the Browns pledge card. Either on the "Connection Sunday" or during the one- to two-week pledge drive period, the two people or couples are to get together for a visit, share with each other about their giving, and then take one another's pledges and return their paired partners' pledge card within the allotted time frame.

I recall how meaningful, and surprising, one such visit was one year. My wife and I had received the card for a newer, younger couple in the church. We got in touch and agreed to get together at their home on an upcoming Sunday night. As it turned out, they lived a good thirty-minute drive from us and we were a little grumpy about driving all the way out there on a dark and rainy Sunday evening when we were tired. Still, we found the place, were welcomed warmly by two of their young children, and sat down for our visit.

We had been given a "discussion guide," which asked that we share with each other an early memory related to money. We did that. The next question invited us to talk about some of our fears and hopes related to money. We did that. Then we were to share what our pledge would be for the coming year and how we had reached that amount. My wife and I shared our pledge for the coming year, feeling good about what seemed to us a significant pledge of $7,000. Our pair said how much they appreciated our pledge and thanked us.

Then it was their turn. Rather quietly they said that they had been moved by a story they had heard in a recent adult education course from which a memorable line had been "Splash it On!" The husband said that they had been fortunate in recent years and they had decided they wanted to "splash it on" this year. They made a pledge of $20,000. My wife and I were fairly stunned. We went home saying to God and one another, "Wow, that was amazing."

The first key step in Each One, Reach One is describing early and often to the congregation how this works, why they are receiving someone else's pledge card in the mail and what they are to do. You'll have to write this, to announce it, to talk about it, and still be prepared to answer questions and correct confusion.

Another key step is preparing a format for discussion for the paired visits. In this format, you do have maximal opportunity to invite people to talk with one another about faith and money. Questions should be open-ended and interesting, such as "Share an early memory of money in your life." "A way or time I've experienced God's presence in our church in the last year . . ." "A story of generosity that touched you . . ." Or provide an inspiring or provocative short quote and ask people to share their thoughts or reactions with each other. People can be encouraged to pray together, and a sample prayer or two provided.

Arranging the pairs is also key. Again, involve in the pairing several people whose knowledge of the congregation and its members is high and ask the pastor(s) to review the pairing. Try to pair people with similar giving potential. Sometimes you want to place people of similar potential giving but different actual giving together so that one can inspire the other. Avoid pairing people with those who are already best friends. Make it an opportunity to get to know someone new.

You may still want to have some trained callers and some specific groups for which you arrange calls rather than paired visits. For example, you might have calls made by experienced and capable callers to all the people who were new members in the last year. They may need this kind of attention and education. Or there may be a whole group of people who can no longer leave their own homes or retirement homes or nursing facility. For these too you may wish to take them out of the paired visit pool and have a group of trained callers.

The strengths of Each One Reach One include getting a high number involved and having face-to-face contacts. You will need good informational and publicity work on the front end, as well as good follow-up for those pairs that for one reason or another don't work. A weakness of the Each One Reach One format is that you may not achieve as high a dollar amount as with the EMSC because it lacks the caller training. And you are likely to have some people, no matter how much explaining you do, who think they have someone else's pledge card "by mistake." Another weakness of EORO is that without the training segment that EMSC has, your opportunity to communicate urgency and enthusiasm in such sessions is lost. Often, as noted earlier, a high percentage of your total support will have come from people who have attended and been moved by that training session component of the EMSC method.

Neighborhood-Meeting-Based Stewardship Drive

In this format you set up a sufficient number of neighborhood meetings that there is one for every fifteen to twenty people in the congregation. You have them at different times (some daytime, some evening) scattered throughout the geographical area of the church. You invite everyone to at least one meeting. At the meeting you have a trained facilitator who is in charge and who leads the meeting (that person is different from the host in whose home you meet).

Components of the meeting may include: discussion of the church's purposes and vision/priorities; conversation in large or small groups in response to the kinds of open-ended questions noted under EORO; prayer; sharing about where we see ourselves going or where people think God is calling us to go as a church; more prayer; personal sharing of joys or concerns; and distribution and completion of pledge cards, or just distribution of the cards at the conclusion with a request to complete them and bring them to church on a particular Sunday or mail them to the church by such-and-such date. You may want to have one dedication Sunday when everyone is asked to bring their completed pledge cards.

Key steps of the Neighborhood Meeting format include identifying host homes that enjoy hosting such gatherings. The hosts are given a list of church members/friends in their area and are asked to call to invite people to come. The hosts have the list of other times and locations. If people cannot come to the neighborhood meeting of the host, the host offers an alternative and contacts the other host with that information.

Another key step is recruiting and selecting the neighborhood meeting facilitator. These should be people who enjoy others, have good people skills, are enthusiastic about the church and its ministry, and have a strong giving pattern and commitment. The training session for facilitators should be well planned and with good information provided. Facilitators should have a list of those invited and expected to attend. The format of the neighborhood gathering should be clear and focused without being rigid.

The strengths of this approach include the following: people often seem to enjoy gathering in homes, whether as hosts or guests. Usually the meeting will include some kind of food, whether potluck dinner or dessert, and people enjoy that too. If the facilitator is comfortable and does a good job, people will enjoy getting to know others and talking together.

Weaknesses of this format are that, again, you have reduced the number of people who benefit from a training experience. And you will tend to reach, for the most part, those who are already committed and active. Those who have become less active or drifted to the fringe are less likely to come out to such a gathering. You will probably, for that reason, end up doing a fair number of your contacts by mail only.

Selective Visitation

Selective Visitation, which was already mentioned under Each One Reach One, is done in combination with one of the other methods, whether Each One Reach One, Neighborhood Meetings, or Mail Canvass. It means that you identify some groups that you, for whatever reason, really want to contact with a home visit, though it will not be the majority of your congregation.

There are three kinds of people or groups that are good candidates for Selective Visitation. One group consists of your highest givers or potential givers. They are most likely to make the greatest increases. If you face significant financial challenges in the coming year, you may wish to selectively visit your ten to twenty highest givers. A variation on this is to have a neighborhood or home gathering for the same group, possibly hosted by the senior minister. A second group that you may wish to target consists of those who have joined the church in the last year. Again, there is special opportunity here. Often newer members have high interest and enthusiasm, and they may be curious about what's expected. Arranging for a visit from a well trained, experienced stewardship caller can be very important and worthwhile. Again, you could do this with a home gathering for everyone who has joined the church in the last year. Finally, there are those with special needs, whom you may wish to refer to as "The VIPs." These may include the frail elderly and shut in. Often these are people who love the church and value the face-to-face connection. Moreover, they want to be kept up to date and not be forgotten.

The upsides of the Selective Visitation include requiring fewer volunteers and visits than EMSC or EORO but still making personal contacts with particular people. The downside is that there are a lot of people you don't reach with a face-to-face visit because you are reaching most people through a larger-group neighborhood meeting or a mail-only contact.

Mail Only Canvass

The Mail Only Canvass is a mail or e-mail solicitation that goes to the home of each member or active friend or family. Each person or family receives one or sometimes two mailings, which include some background material explaining church goals and a pledge card to be completed, signed, and returned. While this is the least intensive and least productive method, it is the one most churches use and which they use year after year.

Key steps here will be good front-end information that is communicated in several different formats, including mailings, e-mail, posters and bulletin boards at church, newsletter information, times of testimony or sharing during worship, and then a stewardship or pledge Sunday when everyone is encouraged to bring their completed pledge card and put it in the offering that Sunday.

Strengths of this approach are that it requires a fairly low number of volunteers and volunteer time. It does require that the volunteers who work on the stewardship program be visible, positive, and encouraging. Another strength of this method, at least from the point of view of some, is that it allows for maximum privacy. The weaknesses, again, are pretty much the flip side of the strengths. You won't reach as many people. You won't move many people to change whatever their existing giving pattern is. You will have to do a fair amount of phone or mail follow-up, as this method allows people to let their pledge get lost in a stack of mail or be thrown out to be recycled.

As I noted in the beginning, we have moved in a descending order in terms of time, effort, and results. Still, there is no one best or right method. Congregations that are doing a capital drive are well advised to do an EMSC or some variation of it. Otherwise, you can probably use any one of these formats for several years and then go to another. For example, you might do the EMSC one year, then do EORO for three years followed by Neighborhood Meetings for one or two years, followed by a return to EMSC or EORO. In the next chapter, we will look at "Putting It All Together," and a sequence of steps that can be applied to one or more of these formats.

Questions for Reflection, Discussion, and Action

1. Assess where you are in the life of your church at the present time. Is there one format that, given your assessment, seems to make the most sense for you at this time?

2. What has been your pattern in recent years? Assess the strengths and weakness of your existing method or approach.

3. Return to a consideration of your church's purpose (mission) and vision (priorities) at present. In light of those, does one of these methods seem to make the most sense and be a good fit? Why?

Eight

Putting It All Together

The goal of this chapter is to give you a blueprint for your stewardship ministry. In providing this blueprint I will have an imagined congregation in mind.** That congregation is one that has not put particular emphasis on stewardship in recent years, perhaps in many years. Oh, there has been a pledge Sunday and perhaps a small group of people working on it. But for the most part it's been a matter of drafting a proposed budget, telling people where the increases are, encouraging people to renew and modestly increase their pledge, and that's about it.

You are reading this book because that's no longer working. Perhaps every year is a struggle to make ends meet. Possibly you've been running deficits for a couple of years and can see that you will soon have exhausted accumulated assets that have been subsidizing the budget. Maybe you have called a new pastor in the last few years and there's new energy in the church. Or you may be getting ready to have your first capital fund drive in some time because you have needs that can no longer be put off. In other words, there is some need, maybe even excitement, about "turning things around."

That's great, a wonderful place to start. But before we get too much further down the road, ponder this question: Would you describe the atmosphere and motivation as one of anxiety or one of urgency? Anxiety tends to be born of fear or worry. When this is the motivation, people say things like,

"If we don't do something soon, this church will close its doors." We may be feeling anxious about survival. Anxiety is part of the human make-up and there's reason for it. It may provide a starting place, but rather quickly we want to try to make a move in our outlook, language, and motivation from anxiety to urgency. Urgency is less fear-driven and more hope-inspired. Here the question is not "Will we survive?" but "How will we take the steps toward thriving?" In and around all of this, let's not so much look to anxiety or fear as our motivator, but to building a sense of urgency and hope. Sometimes those in leadership are experts in anxiety and a survival mentality. Such leaders tend to think their role is not to grow the church's ministry, but to minimize church expenses. If this is the case, you need to get new leaders or convert the ones you have.

So my imagined congregation has been on a plateau, or it has been relatively stable but slowly declining. This is the situation for a significant number of long-established, mainline Protestant congregations. The good news is that new attention to stewardship is a great lever for broad church renewal. Paying fresh attention to stewardship should prompt attention to key questions like "Why are we here?" "What are we trying to accomplish?" "What's our story?" "What are our most important priorities in the next five years?" and "Where do we experience God's presence in our church?"

Paying disciplined attention to stewardship also brings all of these questions—as well as the direction and overall vitality of the church—home to each and every individual and family in the congregation. We're talking here not just about stewardship as money and finances, but our stewardship of the church and the gospel. Eventually each one of us must, in the words of Scripture, "Choose this day whom you will serve" (Josh. 24:15). Each of us faces a decision to grow in the spiritual practices of stewardship and generosity. So there's great leverage for church renewal and vitality in a solid and positive stewardship focus. It addresses us in both our plural "You," that is, the church, and in the singular "You," that is, individually.

If you are seeking to revitalize your congregation, stewardship might not be the place to begin, but it is a key part of an overall renewal package and strategy. In my own view the key steps in church renewal look something like this:

- You start with your pastoral leadership; you have to have a person of real faith and competence here. If you have a staff, they need to be people of faith and competence and be on board as a team together.
- Next you focus on worship, its life and renewal.

- In some congregations, the way decisions are made and power is exercised has become an in-group affair dominated by one or two people or cliques, often in violation of church operating agreements (Constitution and By-Laws). If that's the case, you'll have to work to establish open, by-the-book, transparent, and accountable decision making and governance processes.
- Simultaneously with creating open and accountable decision-making and governance, the pastor engages lay leaders in substantive discussion about purpose (mission) and vision (priorities).
- Now (and the above steps will take several years) you have enough building blocks in place to turn to stewardship. Or you start earlier with stewardship, letting it drive leadership, governance, and worship renewal.

So our imagined congregation has been on a plateau, coasting, or declining slowly. Congregational size matters some in terms of how you go about things, but what I have thus far suggested and will propose can (and has) proven effective in congregations of varying sizes. Generally speaking, smaller congregations are less complex and more relational organizations, while larger congregations tend to be more complex and will support greater structure and complex systems. You have to take account of these dynamics but avoid the temptation to say, "This will never work for us; we're a small church." Or "We already know how to do all this, we're a big church." Whatever your size, if you are lacking vitality and have been coasting, maintaining, or slowly declining, a new focus on stewardship can be both cause and effect of congregational renewal.

In the previous chapter I reviewed five basic options for organizing and conducting your stewardship ministry. In this chapter I want to utilize some of those options in developing a long-term plan for stewardship as a part of overall congregational renewal. Note, I said "long term." Often stewardship programs or capital drive canvasses are conceived as one-year intensives. I want to recommend a longer-term commitment and piece of work because what we are trying to do here is change lives and change the culture of your congregation. That seldom happens in one year. Even if you do well in that one year, it's difficult to sustain the change and new direction unless you've planned for it. So I will give you a couple of options for conceiving a longer-term approach to stewardship, and then I will develop one of those in greater detail.

One option would be to take three of the different approaches described in chapter 7 and utilize them in successive years. So, year one, you do the EMSC; year two, EORO; and year three, a Neighborhood Meeting method. If you are doing a capital drive concurrent with your program in support of your operating budget, this is probably a wise sequence. Alternatively, you might consider a six-year sequence: doing the EMSC for the first two years, EORO in years three and four, and Neighborhood Meetings in years five and six. This has the advantage of allowing learning in the first year and building on and utilizing that learning in the second year of each format.

For the congregation that is seeking overall renewal and greater vitality I would suggest a three-year sequence that would start with the Neighborhood Meeting format in the first year, Each One Reach One in the second year, and then in year three the Every Member Stewardship Canvass. This makes change a little more gradual and gives people a chance to grow into a new or renewed emphasis. Alternatively, you could commit to using any one of the three strategies for three years in a row. But if you conceptualize this as a three-year piece of work, then you are more likely to impact people's lives and change patterns in congregational culture. (Incidentally, you don't stop after three years, but you do think of three years as a period of renewal, redirection, and establishing a foundation. The next three can be thought of as the next chapter.)

In and through all you do, keep clearly in mind that the focus is not the budget, nor is it fund raising. There is rather a dual focus on the congregation's purpose (mission) and on stewardship and generosity as spiritual practices. As described in chapters 2 and 3 these are really two parts of one whole. But what we're after here is not just fundraising. It is more faithfully and fruitfully fulfilling the purpose for which God has called us and helping people grow in the related spiritual practices of stewardship and generosity.

Now I will work through a series of steps in sequence with some guidelines about timing. This schedule will assume the traditional culmination in November.

Step One: As part of overall church renewal and revitalization, your governing board or the congregation itself has decided that renewing/deepening stewardship is a priority. Getting buy-in on this commitment, at least from the leaders, is essential. This happens in November (one year prior to the drive itself), December, or January.

Step Two: Take some "soundings." In other words, create some settings and occasions for conversation. The board chair and pastor might visit some of your larger donors and supporters. Ask them some questions about how they think things are going for the church. Ask what they see as strengths and needs. Indicate that you are exploring a renewed focus on stewardship. Ask for their reactions and ideas.

Or create a think-tank group of twelve to fifteen committed, engaged members (some longtime, some newer, some in-between) and have a similar conversation one evening. This was also described in chapter 5 on leadership strategies under "Defining Reality." You can also sponsor a focus group or two, again exploring similar questions. The idea is to initiate a conversation, get a sense of where people are, what their hopes and concerns are, and what they think is important as your church puts a new emphasis on stewardship. Those who lead these visits, meetings, or conversations should take notes and ask if they may report people's comments (without attribution) to the whole board and to the new stewardship team. Step two is a January project.

Step Three: Step three builds on step two. The pastor and board chair should invite one or two people to head up the new stewardship team. Then when that person or pair is on board, the three or four should pray about and brainstorm names of people for the stewardship team. That group should be made up of ten to fifteen people. If you are a small church and can manage a team of only five to seven, then that's okay too. At the first meeting of the team, you not only thank people for agreeing to take part, but also lay out why this is a priority for the church, how important it is, and, broadly speaking, what you hope to accomplish. People recruited for the team should be strong givers or certainly have the potential to become so. One reason to do the soundings before recruiting the team is that the sounding visits/sessions may help to identify some of those who have interest and insight for this task. Recruitment of the team occurs in February.

Step Four: The team gets underway by developing information. Notes from the sounding sessions should be made available with interpretation by those who conducted the sessions. With help from office staff the team should put together information about stewardship over the last ten years. How many pledges have we had? How many regular givers who do not pledge? How are these numbers changing? How many pledges do you have at different levels? What trends do you see in amounts pledged? Look at your budget as well as year-end actuals for the previous ten years. Also look at the membership and worship attendance figures over the same period. Finally, the team should seek to establish giving potential through a process of income estimation as described earlier. Based on such estimates what is the current overall percent of income giving level of the congregation. What does the team imagine the potential might be?

The team should gather and study all this information, make some observations based on the information and patterns, and see if the group has some preliminary insights or conclusions. Next the team should meet with the governing board to report what it is finding. Discuss the findings with the board. Ask board members for their observations and insights. The team should indicate that the full support of the pastor and board will be essential and ask them to affirm that support at this time. (Generally it is probably wise if the pastor or Senior Minister is essentially part of the new stewardship team and working with that group on an ongoing basis). Step four should be carried out in March and April.

Step Five: During Lent, begin a congregation-wide study of stewardship and generosity as spiritual practices. You could call it "Less Is More" or "How Much Is Enough?" or "Living as Spiritual People in a Consumeristic Society." You may develop a four- or six-week series using the six bible studies in chapter 4 of this book. Or you can use other study resources listed in the Resources section. Or you may draw selectively from this book or others I have used (see the endnotes). The point here is to be intentional about faith formation.

Step Six: In May the stewardship team should decide on the goals (one and three years) for their work. This will include giving goals as well as process goals (e.g., we will use a Neighborhood Meeting format in Year One, hoping to have attendance and participation by 65 percent of our members). The giving goal may be a dollar amount or an overall percentage increase in giving. My recommendation is that the giving goal ("the challenge pledge goal") be the 5 percent "modern tithe" discussed earlier. In May the names of the stewardship team leaders and team members should be announced to the congregation, with some broad-brush indication of the nature of the three-year focus and methods we will be using in the fall. Also at this time, newsletter, website, and bulletin boards should be utilized to communicate "What People Are Thinking," which would mean quotes or statements from the soundings session and initial team meetings. And the team should begin to make available some of the information from the giving analysis. This process of information distribution and communication should be continued over the summer.

Step Seven: In August and September the team should announce and communicate its goals and how the congregation will be asked to participate this fall (Neighborhood Meetings, EORO, or EMSC). Whichever method is chosen, the team will need to work out a further sequence of steps and timing to carry out that method or strategy. In other words, if we are going to have Neighborhood Meetings in October, when do we recruit hosts? make invitation calls? do mailings? If the EMSC format is used, then when in September will callers be recruited and when in October will training sessions be held?

What about a "theme"? The idea of having a theme is popular and fine. But since I am recommending a three-year focus, I would also recommend that the theme be a three-year theme that reflects the overall emphasis that the board and congregation have agreed to place on stewardship and church renewal. In other words, don't pick three different themes, one for each year. Pick one theme for the entire three years, whether "Growing in Giving," "Building for the Future," "Growing in Generosity," "Stewards of God's Gift: the Church," or the like.

Step Eight: Prepare for and carry out in October and/or November whichever method you have chosen. If you've decided to do Neighborhood Meetings this year, then September is the time to plan and recruit, and October is the time to publicize and hold the meetings.

Also at this time you should be creating your pledge cards. Pledge cards should state clearly (1) the challenge pledge goal, (2) the total amount of the pledge and the amount pledged as a weekly sum and (3) a clear statement to the following effect: "A pledge is a statement of intent. Your pledge may be revised at any time should your circumstances change." In other words, and this should be made clear, a pledge is not a legally binding contract. It is a statement of intent, which allows church leaders to plan.

Use newsletters, websites, bulletin boards, and mailings to get out information about giving patterns, goals, and the stewardship program itself. Members of the stewardship team should make a point of being present on Sundays and wear some kind of large, gaudy name tags that indicates they are on the stewardship team and are happy to interpret information and answer questions.

Some congregations, especially those doing a capital drive, will wish to develop a major magazine-like piece that conveys the congregation's purpose and vision, story, and giving goals. It should also have brief letters from the pastor and key leaders, as well as something like "testimonies," or brief statements of personal meaning found in participation in the church and in giving from a range of members. In all of this you keep the focus on the two core messages: the church's purpose/story and growing in the spiritual practices of stewardship/generosity. Remember that people's giving is greatly effected by their "reference group," so encourage some of your strong givers to tell their giving story, how they have arrived at what they do give and what it means to them.

Step Nine: Carry out the program you've decided on, whether Neighborhood Gatherings, EORO or EMSC. This happens in October or November. There can be one "Celebration Sunday" when the calls are made, but it is more likely that you will have two special Sundays as part of the stewardship drive, one that begins the stewardship period and program and another that climaxes it. "Celebration Sunday" should be festive, a great service with a stewardship message, maybe with a brunch and program following. Two weeks later have "Consecration Sunday" or "Harvest Sunday," with another festive service, an offertory procession, and gathering of the pledges. Whichever format you use, remember that those who are providing leadership have already made their pledge and are asking others to join them.

Step Ten: Use newsletters, Sunday service announcements, websites and bulletin boards to report on how you are doing: pledges received and amount pledged. On Celebration Sunday, you should be able to report how many pledges have come from your staff, stewardship team, and those working on the stewardship program. Continue to report on the number of pledges made and the amount pledged. All reports are "Thank you reports," that is, a combination of updates and heartfelt appreciation. You probably should do your final report in early December. This does not mean that you will have all pledges made. There will still be some folks you haven't heard from. A two- or three-person follow-up team does phone call follow-up, or in some cases mailing another pledge card with a handwritten note. As pledges are received in November and December, they should be acknowledged with a letter confirming the amount of the pledge and thanking people for their generous commitment and participation.

Reports should be made in November and December to the stewardship team as a whole and to the governing board. In January the team should meet to evaluate the program, to share experiences and insights, to report findings and results to the board, and to begin to lay plans for Year Two and the method you will use in Year Two. A key part of follow-up is an easy to understand quarterly statement from the church that indicates the amount pledged and the amount received to date with an expression of gratitude and reaffirmation of church purpose. Providing such information quarterly goes a long way to helping people complete their pledge. Failure to provide this information in a timely, comprehensible, and positive way is to invite people to forget or neglect their pledge.

Finally, a note about "little things." In any stewardship ministry or program there are many opportunities to do little things that mean a lot and to do them well. For example, if you are the pastor, the chair of the board, or a leader of the stewardship team, send thank-you notes to those working with you, letting them know how much their participation and partnership means to you. If you are using the EMSC format, team captains should likewise send thank-you notes to those who have agreed to be callers. When the work is done they should send another thank-you note.

Or another example: if you have Celebration Sunday brunch following worship, make it really nice. Put flowers on the tables. Plan for a tasty, attractive, and special menu, not the usual potluck and certainly not pizzas from a nearby pizza joint!

Some other "little things" that matter. If you are mailing out pledge cards or a packet with stewardship materials and pledge cards, don't use mailing labels. Get some members of the team together to hand address the envelopes with a quick "thank you so much" handwritten on the back. Just be thoughtful, and you'll come up with more ways to add the little touches that make a big difference.

You will have noticed in reading this chapter that part of what makes a new or renewed emphasis on stewardship succeed is that you don't try to do it all in one month, or worse, one or two weeks. You work at this over the course of a year. And you do this in ways that involve a growing number of people in conversation, in receiving information, and in playing a part, whether large or small, in the total venture. Instead of "quick and dirty" we're aiming for "strong and steady." Instead of stewardship that aims to enable the church to survive or scrimp by for another year, we are working to help the church thrive and flourish for the future. We want to give members and friends of the congregation a real chance to grow in the practice of being generous givers. Perhaps as you read this chapter you have thought, "That's a lot of work!" Yes, it is. Do tailor and adapt these ideas to your setting. But don't expect progress without work and commitment.

Questions for Reflection, Discussion, and Action

1. What parts of this overall plan excite you? What parts concern you?

2. How do you respond to the suggestion of developing a three-year plan?

3. Can you turn this series of steps into a work plan or spreadsheet tied to the calendar?

Nine

The Three-Legged Stool

The previous two chapters on conducting your stewardship ministry only
addressed giving in support of a congregation's normal or annual operating budget. This chapter aims to expand our ideas about ways congregations are supported financially and the ways people give. While the operating
budget has traditionally gotten most of our focus, to imagine that the operating budget will do it all is probably not helpful or accurate. The concept of the
three-legged stool helps to expand our thinking.

In order to stand, a stool needs three legs. One leg or even two doesn't
work. You need three legs, preferably of equal lengths, for the thing to work.
Congregations might think in terms of three "legs" of financial support. The
first leg, the focus of much discussion to this point, is the pledging and giving in support of the annual operating budget. The second leg is planned
giving, which means people's inclusion of the church in their estates through
their wills, but also includes vehicles that allow people to make a gift in their
lifetime (charitable remainder trusts, annuities, and the like). Planned Giving
establishes and supports an endowment. The third leg of the stool is periodic
capital drives, which fund buildings and capital improvements.

It's important to note that people will often draw on different sources
for their giving to these various "legs." Giving to the operating budget is by
and large done from people's ongoing annual income. Planned giving to an

endowment is often done from a person or family's accumulated assets (savings, annuities, real estate, stocks). And giving to capital drives is often a combination of the two sources, annual income and accumulated assets.

Having focused on the stool's first leg already, let's turn to the second and third, planned giving for endowments and capital fund drives.

Both clergy and laity tend to have mixed feelings about endowments. (Just to be clear, an "endowment" is, by definition, a fund that maintains in perpetuity the fund's principal while making the income earned from the principal available for present uses.) People's mixed feelings about endowments find expression in remarks such as the following: "Endowments kill churches." "They are a church of fat cats, sitting on a huge endowment."

Endowments do represent a challenge, and it is true that some churches with significant endowments have declined. But I'm not sure the problem lies with the endowment itself. Usually the problem is the loss of a sense of purpose or mission, along with an absence of clear vision or priorities. When leadership and congregation aren't doing their job by holding a clear and compelling purpose and vision, then an endowment allows a false sense of security and a well-funded decline. The problem in a general way is sinful human nature and in a particular way the failure of a clear sense of purpose and vision. If those, purpose and vision, are in place and strong, then an endowment merely provides more money for more mission and ministry. As noted earlier, too many of those in church leadership seem to believe that their job is to minimize expenses instead of maximizing ministry. When that's the case an endowment tends to be counterproductive. To be sure, an endowment does represent a challenge and opportunity that not all congregations are prepared to use well. Some congregations are like the servant in the parable of the talents (Matt. 25:14–30) . They are frightened of opportunity and risk and prefer to bury what has been entrusted to them. Often, then, like the hapless servant they end up losing even that.

But some other congregations resemble the first or second servant in that same parable. Entrusted with a great resource, they are eager to use it in service of their master. They understand what the Gospel of Luke says in summing up the significance of several parables of stewardship (Luke 12:35–47): "From everyone to whom much has been given, much will be required; and from the one to whom much has been entrusted, even more will be demanded" (Luke 12:48). Some, perhaps all of us at times, shrink from such challenge. Fear and distrust diminish us and distort our lives and churches. But the most vital congregations are not bound by fear. They are able to take wise risks in faith and to be found worthy of trust, capable of using well the gifts and resources entrusted to them. But again this takes us back to our beginning point, our capacity to know and express an overarching sense of purpose and to build from that purpose a vision for the present.

There are other reasons for congregations to develop or continue to build this second leg of the three-legged stool. Today in many congregations of the United Church of Christ as well as other mainline Protestant bodies, members do have accumulated assets in the form of real estate, stocks, annuities, and the like. Sometimes people find that they have assets far beyond their expectations or needs. When churches have a planned giving program they can offer their members the opportunity to consider and discuss the stewardship of these assets, which is an important thing to do. How are my accumulated assets to be used? Can the values that shaped my life and giving in my lifetime also shape the use of my assets after I die? Can our assets continue our support and stewardship for concerns and causes that have been important to us during our lifetime? These are important questions to ask. Simply giving a large amount to one's children is not always the best idea, even for those children. A church performs a service to its people by raising such questions and giving people opportunities to use their assets wisely and in ways that are in keeping with their faith and values.

Building on this, a planned giving ministry and an endowment also provide a way for a congregation to have a real sense of its past and of the generations that have gone before the present one. In one congregation I served we held an annual event in celebration of those who had given to build the church's endowment as well as those who had indicated that they had made a provision for the church in their will or estate plans. We put on a nice dinner, had some good music and a good speaker. We also spent some time, at each such dinner, hearing about one or two of the "saints now departed" who had contributed to the endowment. We recalled their story, their loves and passions, and had a display of photos and other memorabilia. We remembered the ways they participated in the church and the wider community. We would also do similar "feature stories" in the church newsletter and on the website, recalling such individuals, their character and legacy. This made for a memorable, often poignant, evening at the annual dinner and celebration. It also enriched the life of the church as we remembered, with gratitude, those who had gone before us.

And just in case you are thinking, "Well, that discriminates in favor of the wealthy," that's not really true. That congregation's substantial endowment had been built from many, many small gifts. The average bequest was $11,000, but some were $1,000 or even less. They came not from the extremely wealthy, but from people of average means who had worked as schoolteachers, social workers, in small businesses of their own, and so on. One thing we stressed at the dinner celebration was that really any of us can do this. I think this was one factor that gave that particular congregation a real sense of its past as a strength and resource. After all, those who had gone before us had not given to the endowment to keep a dying church on life-support. They had given to it because they wanted the church to serve vital values with courage and creativity.

A secondary benefit of an endowment is that it may help a congregation to be honest and real about an important truth, namely, that most Christians in the first world are "rich Christians," when considered in a global context. We live in a world where some have a great deal of wealth, even if they are not "wealthy" by the standards of their own community, while many more live in great poverty. Paradoxically, a congregation that is not afraid of money and has an endowment is perhaps in a better position to speak honestly about these realities than the church that lives hand-to-mouth and prefers, like the third servant in the parable of the talents, to hide from its own reality and resources.

Here's a simple suggestion for planting the concept of planned giving with members and friends of your congregation. On your regular pledge card have a line with a check-off box that reads, "I have remembered [name of church] in my estate plan or will." Some people will have done that, and you can record their names and thank them. Others will not have done that, but seeing it on the pledge card may get them thinking about doing so. You can also put a similar note in your church newsletter. "Remember [name of church] in your will or estate plan." Again, this may be reenforced with an occasional newsletter article about someone who made such a gift and, who is no longer with us, but whom we remember with gratitude. As others read such articles they will not only remember the person whose story is being told; they may think, "I want to do that too."

Some churches or leaders hesitate to create an endowment because of the responsibilities entailed in managing such a fund. But don't let that stop you. The United Church of Christ, and other denominations, offer management services for little or no cost. You can pool your church's endowed funds with those of other congregations and have them managed for you.

Rather than making the church scrimp by, we do better to claim what has been entrusted to us and use it well and boldly in service of God and God's dream of a restored creation. Many of our congregations need a larger vision. They need to be touched by the spirit that animated the prophet Isaiah, who was continually saying things like, "Awake, awake, put on your strength, O Zion!" and "Shake yourself from the dust, rise up, O captive, Jerusalem" (Isa. 52:1–2)

The third leg of the three-legged stool is the capital drive. A capital drive, again by definition, is undertaken to restore or build fixed assets, "bricks and mortar," buildings and facilities. If the operating budget and the income earned from an endowment support the ongoing ministry or program, the capital drive builds or restores the structure that houses or is the base of operations for the ongoing ministry.

Some churches are reluctant to consider or undertake capital drives. Some clergy and other church leaders also would rather avoid them. As a young minister I fell into that category simply because of inexperience. As I mentioned in the first chapter, as a pastor, I've been part of three capital drives during my ministry, and I can honestly say that every one of them has been a good experience for me personally and professionally. Moreover, each has been a good experience, even a transformative one, for the congregation.

How so? Capital drives ordinarily represent a challenge. They ask us key questions, "Why are we here?" "What are we trying to accomplish?" "Can we make a compelling case?" "What is our vision for the future of this church and its ministry?" These are important questions to ask, questions that in the best of all situations are continually before a congregation. When they have, however, slipped off our radar and we have moved into a maintenance or stable-but-declining mode, the advent of a capital drive can renew energy and restore urgency. This is not to say that we take on a capital drive without good reason. It is to say that we ought not shrink from doing so when the need exists.

And, often today, the need exists. So many church buildings of the once mainline have been neglected and allowed to deteriorate. You know how it is to visit the home of some aged family members? You can see that things were once kept up and nice, but they have taken on the look and feel, sometimes the odor, of a not very interesting or much visited museum. The truth is that too many of our church buildings have that look and feel. They say "yesterday" or "neglect" or "museum" rather than "today" or "confidence" or "vital mission and ministry." In not a few cases, maintenance needs are put off year after year, until the bill has become so large that a congregation can't begin to tackle it and must close.

Again, the important thing is not the building itself. It is the sense of purpose and mission and the vision and priorities for ministry and service. The building is in service to these and not an end in itself. In this sense a building is like a budget. Both are means to the end, which is the purpose or mission. Sometimes congregations do put lavish amounts into care and maintenance of a building but without a clear or compelling sense of mission. Building maintenance becomes the mission. In that instance they may be like a person who is all dressed up with no place to go. Putting the purpose and vision first may mean renovating existing facilities.

It may even mean stepping out of your existing facility or building to build a new or renewed one that fits your present and future mission. Not a few congregations are like David trying to battle in Saul's armor (1 Sam. 17:38 ff.) King Saul insisted that young David wear his armor to take on the fearsome giant, Goliath. When David had it all on he discovered he could barely move, that for him Saul's armor was a cumbersome misfit. "I cannot walk with these . . ." "So David removed them. Then he took his staff in his hand, chose five smooth stones from the wadi and put them in his shepherd's bag," and went off on his mission. (1 Sam. 17:39–40). Some congregations today are trying to engage a twenty-first-century mission while wearing the equivalent of Saul's armor, a building that was just fine in the nineteenth or twentieth century. Some congregations can renovate existing buildings to be better suited to their current life and mission. Other congregations need to consider making their old building into a "heritage chapel" for weddings and funerals and building a new building that is ready for action and is located where God calls the church to be today.

Whether the job is keeping the church building fresh and inviting, bringing it up to date for today's mission, or building a new building for a new time, a capital drive will be necessary. Again, in my own experience a capital drive provides a wonderful occasion for thinking through the big questions, for stirring a sense of urgency, for challenging a congregation to examine its stewardship, and for experiencing real transformation in its life and giving. And it is also a great deal of work! Don't undertake a capital drive lightly, but don't shrink from undertaking it at all. Usually a congregation is well advised to engage the services of a fund-drive consultant when entering into a capital drive.

One further thing to be said of the third leg of the stool, the capital drive: If a planned giving program serves to keep a church aware of its past, of the generations that have gone before, and of "the great cloud of witnesses" gathered about and cheering the current generation on (Heb. 12:1), a capital drive provides an opportunity for a new generation to make its mark and to become stakeholders. A new generation gets the opportunity that previous generations enjoyed. They get to ask, "What facilities do we need?" They "buy-in" as they fund building and restoration work. In my experience of capital drives, they have provided new and younger members of a congregation this opportunity and thus "cemented" their commitment and sense of being a part of the church. Thus, in a certain sense, the three legs of the stool correlate with our experience of time and its dimensions: the past (planned giving); the present (operating budget), and future (capital drive).

How often should churches have "periodic" capital drives? Well, you do need to have a solid reason or "case," whether it is a new building or a major renovation of an existing one. Sometimes too a capital drive may build another facility, whether for youth or family ministry or for a social service mission of the congregation. In any event the need should be real. If the need is real and demonstrable, I would think that capital drives ought to occur not more often than every ten years and not less often than every twenty years.

These days too many mainline Protestant congregations do seem to resemble that timid third servant in Matthew's parable of the talents. We are a little afraid. We choose to bury the gifts entrusted to us rather than boldly put them into play and into service. That parable is in many ways a haunting, cautionary tale. The servant who thought he was "playing it safe" turned out to have made a very unwise and unsafe choice. In the end he lost everything and was cast (horrors) "into the outer darkness." I know, that's harsh! But the point is that playing it safe doesn't keep things safe. He who seeks to save his own life loses it, while the person (and church) who "loses" his or her life for Christ and the gospel ends up saving it (see Mark 8:35).

Questions for Reflection, Discussion, and Action

1. Does your church have a planned giving program and endowment?

2. If you do, how would you say the endowment is viewed? Are people well informed about it? Is it celebrated and viewed as a source of strength? Or is it veiled in secrecy and "buried"?

3. When was your congregation's last capital drive? What kind of experience was it for the church? Good? Not so good?

4. If your congregation were to build and strengthen its own "three-legged stool," who in your current organization should take the lead? Are there denominational staff or consultants who would be helpful to you?

5. What thoughts, concepts, or insights in this chapter were most suggestive or provocative to you? Why?

Ten

Stewardship and the New Technology

Not long ago a coaching client of mine, a thirty-something Disciples of Christ pastor, was slow in making a payment. Her explanation? "I had a hard time finding my checkbook—I just don't write checks anymore." How does she pay for things? Plastic. Debit card or credit card, mostly the former. While our organization, Congregational Leadership Northwest (www.clnorthwest.org), is set up to accept online debit and credit card payment, my coaching/consulting practice is not. Maybe I'd better change that?

The larger point is that, while earlier generations by and large handled things as cash or personal check transactions, and sometimes gifts of stock, younger generations rely less and less on those mediums of exchange. This presents both challenges and opportunities to churches. Here are some suggestions on adapting to these changes and to the possibilities provided by newer technologies.

In terms of regular pledges I would give people the option of an automatic monthly account deduction from their bank account. It can be a choice offered on your pledge card under "Method of Payment."

The automatic deduction does, however, raise some theological and liturgical questions that need to be addressed. If giving is handled as an automatic account deduction, how does a person participate in the act of offering in worship? Giving to God and to God's work through the church is more than a contribution; it is an offering. Offering is something we humans need to experience and to do in our relationship with God. Ultimately, it is ourselves that we offer, our financial gifts being a sign and symbol of our work and of ourselves.

One option for the person who has opted for the automatic deduction is to offer a symbolic $1.00 in a pledge envelope as a way of participating in the act of offering. Another is to have cards in the pews that allow people to offer something else to God, a pledge of time, a hurt they want to turn over to God, a prayer to be placed before God. It is important to continue the practice of offering, to distinguish it from a contribution, and to interpret the act of offering theologically.

Churches ought to consider accepting debit and credit cards, not in the offering plate of course, but as a service of the church office. There are some financial implications to this, as most credit card companies take a percentage for each transaction. There are also some financial management implications. Some Christians and churches, led by Christian financial guru Dave Ramsey, ritually destroy credit and debit cards as a way of helping people say no to overextending themselves in spending and borrowing. So there's a pastoral question to be looked at here.

Another primary way that churches can utilize newer technologies in relation to giving and stewardship is through the use of their website. The evidence is pretty clear that for the majority of people today a church's website is an early point of contact for those who are seeking a church or just curious. Having a great website is important and worth the investment.

I suggest churches consider three possible categories of giving through their websites. When there is a catastrophe, a Hurricane Katrina, an earthquake in Haiti, or a tsunami in Indonesia, people want to help and to respond. Put a "Donate Now" button on your homepage for such needs, explaining how the money will be used or to what agencies it will be directed. For Protestants, Church World Service should remain a first option for disaster relief. Oxfam and World Vision are other reliable choices.

A second use for a website is the periodic special offering, such as the Christmas Offering to aid the homeless in the community or a fund like the United Church of Christ's Veterans of the Cross. It's important not to have too many of these special offerings, lest you cut into support for the church's operating budget or give the impression that "the church is always asking for money." Frame these as opportunities to make a difference in relation to particular needs. The church helps givers by having done the work of "vetting" recipients, making sure that funds are well used without exorbitant overhead expense.

My experience is that four special offerings a year is about right, perhaps one on World-Wide Communion Sunday for global causes, one at Christmas for local needs, another at Lent as part of the spiritual practice of almsgiving (Matt. 6), and another on Easter Sunday. More than that is too much. You could go with one less, three special offerings, but not fewer. It is important to target specific needs and create these opportunities on a thoughtful basis. Then use your website for people to participate in the special offerings, with a feature page on the recipients and a "Donate Now" click on.

Finally, consider a button for a general donation to your church somewhere on your website. There are times, one hopes, when your congregation will come to the attention of the wider community, even the nation, for a stand on an issue, a response to a challenge, or a particular ministry. There will be people in the wider community checking the church's website who will want to offer a tangible sign of support. Help them with a "Donate Now" click-on button.

There are other people who listen weekly to the podcast of the sermons from your church but who live hundreds or thousands of miles away. You can have a friendly invitation to support the church on the sermon page of your website: a "Donate Now" button.

Again, it's important not to overdo this. It's also important that your website is well managed and up-to-date. You don't want content or donation invitations on your site for things that are out-of-date.

Further uses for newer technologies in relation to stewardship and giving are being discovered, some utilizing social networking sites. But these are some of the basics. The point, chiefly, is that the church offer a variety of ways in which people are able to give—including those that are most comfortable for Internet-savvy generations—and not rely entirely on cash or check. To do so would be comparable to insisting that your grandparents' generation must do all its giving by bartering a chicken or a quart of milk. Worked once, but no longer.

And it remains important to balance these varied forms of giving with interpreting the theological meaning of an offering to God as an expression of our worship, devotion, love, and commitment.

Eleven

Stewardship FAQ

In this final chapter I offer brief responses to Frequently Asked Questions and, where pertinent, an indication of the chapter of the book in which you'll find more on this topic.

Q. How much should I give to the church?

A. Enough that it makes a difference in your life. As a guideline I have suggested 5 percent of your income to the church and 5 percent to other causes, groups, and programs also doing God's work in the world (5 percent equals $1 a week for each $1,000 of annual income). For more see Chapter three.

Q. Do endowments kill churches?

A. No, endowments don't kill churches; people do. Endowments sometimes create a false sense of security that results in congregations and their leaders not having a compelling or challenging vision of the church's purpose and potential. That kills churches. See chapter 9.

Q. Should the pastor know how much members give?

A. Yes. If, as I believe, our use of money and our practices of giving and generosity are a barometer of our spiritual condition, a pastor who is charged with the care of the spiritual health of a congregation and the people who make it up should be knowledgeable about the giving patterns of church members. See chapters 5 and 6.

Q. What about "targeted" or "ear-marked" giving? Should people in the church be able to give just to the ministries or projects they care about most?

A. Yes and no. Yes, of course people should be able to give *additional* gifts in support of particular ministries, needs, and projects they care about. The "no" is that "gift" implies letting go without strings attached. Giving *only* to what we want to support or care most about is a way of attaching strings and may be more about control than generous giving. So everyone should be encouraged to pledge and give to the overall operating budget which supports the whole life and ministry of the church and then make additional gifts for specific ministries if they wish.

Q. How many "special offerings" should a church have in a year?

A. By special offerings I mean things like the denominational offerings "Neighbors in Need" and "One Great Hour of Sharing," as well as special offerings taken in response to a local, national, or global crisis or disaster. Sometimes churches do too many of these which makes for confusion. I think four special offerings a year is about the limit, with maybe one additional for a particular, urgent need or disaster response. (Note that One Great Hour of Sharing does create funds that are used for disaster response by Church World Service).

Q. How does the church spend the money I give?

A. Wisely, I hope! It is important that churches and their leaders can answer such questions with accurate and accessible financial statements showing how money given to the church is used. It is common that 60 percent of a church's budget goes to pay clergy and other staff, which translates into all the various programs and ministries offered by a congregation. Churches should be careful to see that money is managed well, that at least two sets of eyes are on all transactions, that the board regularly reviews the financial condition, and that an audit is done by a reputable firm periodically.

Q. How much should the pastor be involved in the stewardship campaign?

A. The pastor should be completely in support of a church's stewardship campaign, should be working alongside its lay leadership, and should bring his or her particular knowledge (of Scripture, theology, and the congregation) to that work. A pastor that takes a "hands-off" attitude communicates that money isn't an appropriate concern of Christian faith and usually undermines a congregation's stewardship. At the same time, the pastor should be "out in front" only sparingly and strategically. See chapter 6.

Q. Why are pledges important?

A. A pledge is a statement of intention, how much a person or family plans to give in support of God's work through the church in the coming year. A pledge is not a legal contract and can be altered if a person's circumstances change. Having a congregation's pledges allows church leaders to plan for the year ahead, to know what they can undertake in that year in ministry and mission.

Q. Does pledging increase giving?

A. Yes, especially if you can get people to consider their pledge on a weekly basis. In other words, writing one $500 check at the end of the year may seem like a big gift. If you figure out what that translates to on a weekly basis, it is a bit less than $9.80 a week, which with an annual income of $50,000 is less than 1 percent giving or, with $100,000 is less than .05 percent giving. However people pay their pledge it's important to encourage looking at what it means on a weekly and monthly basis. Pledging is basically a way of being intentional about our stewardship and generosity.

Q. What do you think about pledging Time, Talent, and Treasure, or surveys that ask people to make commitments in all three areas?

A. Generally, they are a bad idea. They confuse the issue (and the people) and distract from the core questions of how we steward money and grow in the practice of generosity. To be sure, what people offer to God and the church in time and talent is important. But I prefer to work at this in other ways and at other times, for example, through a program and workshops on Gifts Discernment and Discovery. If you do ask people to pledge time and talent, you have to be prepared to process the information and follow up on it. Many churches don't do that follow through, which results in people becoming indifferent and disinterested. I think it best to acknowledge that stewardship has to do with all of life, but during the stewardship program we are focusing on use of money and financial generosity. Other matters will be attended to in other ways at other times.

Q. What's the best stewardship method?

A. The method that is straightforward, clear, inviting, and positive and that encourages people to grow in faith and the spiritual practices of stewardship and generosity. In other words, there is not "one" best method. In chapter 7, I review five different methods, assessing the strengths and weaknesses of each. Which method is best depends on the situation, history, needs, and goals of your congregation. There is no method that is "magic" or that will work without our own commitment and hard work.

Q. How do you teach stewardship to children?

A. In a general way, you teach stewardship by living and talking about the concept that all we have (life, our body, family, the creation, money, friends) has been entrusted us and that God wants us to take good care of it. Life is good; use it well. When it comes to money, give children an age-appropriate amount to put in the offering at church, saying that this is way of remembering God who loves us and remembering other people who need our help. Without overdoing it, parents should find ways to communicate to their children that they find meaning and joy in being generous and that they hope their children will grow up to be generous too.

Q. Should the pastor ever talk or preach about money? If yes, how often?

A. Scripture is a good guide. Jesus talked about money. He seems to have done so fairly often, but contextually. That is, he talked about money when and as it came up in life. And he understood money as part of our overall life and in relationship to our faith.

One to three sermons a year on money and its place in our society, our lives, and our faith seems about right. If you talk about any one subject either all the time or never, you are giving a message. Often pastors do best when they focus on two things. What does Scripture or Jesus teach or say? (And how do they say it?) And pastors should be honest about their own life, their own experiences with money, and their struggles with regard to money. Don't get up in the pulpit to talk about money to others if you haven't thought, prayed and made choices about how you use money in your own life. This doesn't mean you need to be a perfect model. In fact, if you are tempted to present yourself as some kind of "model" you should probably think twice. Speak honestly, with humility, joy, and conviction. See chapters 3, 4 and 6.

Q. Should I teach tithing?

A. Tithing (giving 10 percent) is a great lifelong discipline that I encourage. But I think the place to start is often with the concept of proportionate giving, that is, giving a regular portion or percentage of what has been entrusted to you. Get that concept planted in people's mind and hearts. Consider using the "modern tithe": 5 percent to God and God's work through the church; 5 percent to other causes, charities, programs and institutions that do God's work in the world.

Here's a little "show and tell" to teach proportionate giving. Where I live, apples and potatoes are big. Once or twice at the Celebration Sunday program (see chapter 8) I would come out wearing a chef's apron and hat, equipped with a cutting board, a big knife, and a bag of twenty big Washington apples or Idaho potatoes. I would pile up the twenty and say, "It all belongs to God. God has entrusted it to you. God wants you to keep this much (take away two potatoes or apples, leaving eighteen) for your needs and those of your family. This much (two potatoes) you are to give to God and your neighbors in need."

Taking one potato I would say, "I encourage you to join me in giving this much to God and God's work through the church. This one potato equals 5 percent of the total. Only one potato."

Next, I would cut the potato in half, saying, "Half a potato equals 2.5 percent." Then, still smiling, I would cut the half a potato into slices and hold up a slice. "But some of us [mock sad face] are giving just a potato chip [or French fry] to the Lord!" If the Lord has blessed you with $100,000 a year, $500 is this, a potato chip, a couple of French fries for Jesus!" I would then pick up the half potato and say, "If you've been giving a potato chip, let's try to move to half a potato, 2.5 percent this year. Then maybe in a year or two, you can move to this much, to 5 percent." I would say this as I held up one potato (or apple).

The sight of the pastor wielding a big knife seemed to interest folks. And it was a good object lesson. Of course, it has to be done playfully, and you have to have a good time doing it, and let others have a good time too. If you're angry at the congregation or feeling like the grim reaper, don't do this skit!

Q. Is physical health or fitness part of stewardship? How about care of the earth?

A. Absolutely! While stewardship of our body and creation is not the primary focus of the stewardship drive, at times it should be a focus of the church. More than we tend to, churches need to speak honestly, especially in this time of rising obesity, of taking care of your body. And in the era of climate change, we need to speak of creation care. Too often we say very little about the body in church, assuming a false dichotomy of body and spirit or heaven and earth. Scripture doesn't do that! Paul in particular teaches that the body is the temple of the Holy Spirit and we have an obligation to take care of the temple so that it is fit and ready for God's use.

Q. Should people who are visiting a church or who have come a few times but haven't become members be asked to pledge?

A. Those who have come regularly for three months or more should be included in a church's stewardship program or mailings. If someone is calling on them for stewardship, that should be a specially trained person who is comfortable and knowledgeable about the overall church and how stewardship fits in here. I would suggest the caller make the visit an option by saying something like, "We would like to include you in our stewardship program this year if you are comfortable with that. And I would love to visit and talk with you about the church and how you can participate. If you're not ready for that at this time, that's fine. We're so glad you are worshiping with us and look forward to growing together."

Q. Is it wrong to ask someone who doesn't have much money for a pledge?

A. No. In fact, what may be really bad is to figure, "She doesn't have much; let's skip her," or "They're having a hard time right now; we shouldn't call on them." The message that gives people may be that they don't matter, that what they have to offer isn't important, or that they aren't really a part of the church. It is very important to include everyone, and let people decide what is right for them to do. You can point out that a pledge can be revised if need be. Jesus was very clear that what looks to some like a small gift or offering may be a very large one (Mark 12:41–44). Moreover, it is generally true that people who have less are proportionately more generous than the wealthy.

Q. In reference to giving a percentage of income, is it gross or net income that you consider?

A. People always ask this. I say, "You figure that out in conversation with God. Pray about it."

Q. What is the average percent of income UCC members give to their church?

A. People who work in stewardship for the UCC tell me that it is 1.5 percent. The bad news is that our giving level is pretty low. The good news is that we do have room to grow and that the giving potential of most, if not all, UCC churches is much greater than their present actual giving level.

Sometimes when people in a congregation say that they want their church to be more alive, more vital, and to make a bigger difference, I say, "Great. Then what we need for you to do is to put your money where your mouth is and give your church the resources it needs. If the current giving level nationally and in your church is 1.5 percent, and you make a commitment to moving to 5 percent, I *guarantee* that your church will become stronger, more vital, and will make a much greater difference in your community and world.

Q. How do you respond when someone says they are happy to give some time to the church but they can't or won't give money?

A. "Thank you. It's great to have your generous gift of time. What, specifically, would you like to be involved in at this time?" Then, add, "I have found that generous financial giving has really been an important part of my life and faith. When you're ready to talk about that, I hope we can have a further conversation."

Q. How should you respond when someone says, "The church is always talking about money?"

A. Assuming that this is a diversionary tactic and not accurate, say, "I don't experience it that way myself. I actually appreciate that our church gives me the opportunity and encouragement to think about how I use the money God has entrusted to me. And I am really excited about what our church is doing. I'd like to invite you to join me in giving that makes a difference in your life." If they still aren't interested or have other excuses, then say thank you and move on (see Luke 10:10–12).

Excuses that people have for not giving—"The church cares only about money," "The church just wastes money when it gets it," "That church has a big endowment," "It's a difficult economy," and many more—need to be recognized for what they are, namely, *excuses*. They are exercises in pocketbook protection. Pastors, stewardship team members, and callers shouldn't be confrontational. But neither should you coddle people or accept their excuses at face value. If a response is merited, respond briefly and then move on to say something like, "I'd like to invite you to join me in the giving to God and God's work through the church. Our challenge pledge goal is . . ."

Q. "I'll do anything but ask people for money" is something that people sometimes say when asked to take part in a stewardship program. How do you respond to that?

A. My answer is, "We don't want you to ask people for money; we do want you to share your own faith and commitment, and to invite others to join you." You can also make this a role play situation at your training. See chapters 7 and 8. Try to unhook people from the idea that they are "asking for money," and instead connect them to (1) sharing what they are doing and (2) inviting people to take part in the church's life and to grow in generosity.

Appendix One

Important Scriptures for Discerning Purpose

These passages can be the basis of a sermon series or adult study on the purpose or mission of the church. In most instances I cite one or two verses, but these should always be studied in context.

Genesis 12:1–4. God begins God's reclamation project, calling Abram and Sar'ai as the father and mother of God's people. Note that God promises to bless them that they might be a blessing to all people. How does that describe and illuminate the nature and purpose of the church?

Leviticus 19:1–2. (also consider all of Leviticus 19). Called the "Holiness Code," this chapter describes the vocation of Israel as being "holy" because God is holy. What does that mean in terms of a way of life and role in relation to others?

Matthew 5:13–16. Jesus in the Sermon on the Mount speaks of the church as the "salt of the earth," and "light of the world." What do these images tell us about the church?

Matthew 28:16–20. In his final words to his disciples, Jesus gives them a charge. What are they to do?

John 20:19–23. The risen Christ charges his disciples, "As God has sent me, so I send you." Who sends them? Who are they sent to? For what purpose?

Acts 1:7–8. "You shall be my witnesses," the risen Christ says to the apostles. What does it mean to be a witness? What does it mean to be a witness to the resurrection?

1 Corinthians 12:12. Paul speaks of the church as the Body of Christ, which is characterized by unity (one body) and diversity (many members). What does this metaphor suggest about the nature and purpose of the church?

1 Peter 2:9–10. Peter piles up different images to speak of the church and its mission. He also locates the church's origins in God's grace.

Appendix Two

Purpose Statements: Criteria and Examples

Definition of a Purpose (Mission) Statement: One succinct, memorable sentence that describes what God has called a church to do. The purpose is a church's God-given reason for being. It will answer the question "Why are we here?"

Criteria for a Good Purpose Statement
- It will be biblically informed and theologically sound but in accessible, everyday language.
- It will fit a particular congregation though need not be unique to it.
- It will generate "lift," that is, be compelling and exciting (without being grandiose or unrealistic).
- It will be short enough that it can be committed to memory and easily displayed and used.

Sample Purpose Statements
- "In every way, in every setting, we seek Growth in Faith"
- "To grow people of faith who participate in God's work in the world."
- "To experience and share abundant life."
- "To extend the reach of Jesus Christ."
- "To welcome people to faith, to equip people with a faith that works in the real world, and to send people into the world to serve in Christ's name."
- "To be a community where Spirit and service come together."
- "To grow people in a faith that does justice, loves kindness, and walks humbly with God."
- "To be and make disciples of Christ."
- "To change lives, to change the world."

Appendix Three

Outline of a Process for Formulating Church Purpose

1. Ask the governing board to create a team to manage your church's process for discerning purpose.

2. Formulate a clear charge for the team, indicating how the governing board is to be kept informed.

3. Use Scriptures in Appendix One as basis of a sermon series or board study.

4. Learn about discernment as a spiritual practice. I recommend the Alban book by Danny Morris and Chuck Olsen, *Discerning God's Will Together.*

5. In a variety of settings in the life of the church ask people to reflect on the following questions:

   (a) Where do you sense God's presence in the life of our church today?

   (b) Where do you sense God is calling us to go in the future?

6. Create occasions where you have "max-mix groups," i.e., groups with as great as possible diversity in age, length of time in the church, church background, gender, race/ethnicity. Explore the two questions above (*a* and *b*) in these groups. (Note: when people talk only in well-established groups they tend to have their own opinion reenforced and miss other perspectives. Hence max-mix.)

7. The team listens, gathers information, prays, waits on the Spirit, and drafts a purpose statement to present first to the governing board and then to the congregation. Feedback is invited.

8. If necessary the team revises the statement in light of feedback and then presents it to the board or congregation or both for approval.

9. Leaders of the church use the statement in communication, planning, identity building, development of vision, leadership training, new member orientation, publicity, and evaluation.

Appendix Four

"Then and Now"

Developed by a group of church leaders with whom I worked in New England (with some additions of my own, particularly with regard to stewardship), these comparisons can help us to name and understand better our "New Time."

Then: Every respectable and upwardly mobile citizen was expected to be in church on Sunday morning.

Now: Society at large cares little if someone attends worship or not.

Then: Stores were closed on Sundays.

Now: Sunday is the second busiest shopping day of the week.

Then: When individuals moved into a new community, one of the first things they did was join a church.

Now: If someone decides to join a church, it is only after a long process of deliberation and church shopping.

Then: The phrase "Under God" was added to the Pledge of Allegiance and prayers were routinely offered in the public schools.

Now: Prayer is forbidden at all public school events, including graduation.

Then: Baptism was by and large baptism of infants. It was "expected" as a family and social ritual. Preparation consisted largely of communicating the logistics of the ceremony.

Now: Increasingly, baptism is also of adults, is consciously chosen and prepared for with a course of study.

Then: The focus of church mission efforts was denominationally sponsored foreign missions.

Now: The focus of church mission outreach is "hands-on" efforts, often but not always in the local community.

Then: A civic organization was expected to have at least one clergyman on its board, and would invite him to offer prayer before the meeting.

Now: A civic organization may have a clergyperson on its board but would not ask him or her to offer prayer.

Then: The authority of the pastor of a local church was widely recognized in the community, as well as within the local church.

Now: The authority of the pastor of a local church is recognized only within the church (and sometimes not even there!).

Then: The role of the laity was to help ministers to minister.

Now: The role of the clergy is to equip laity for their ministry.

Then: Sermons preached from "important pulpits" were often quoted or reviewed in Monday morning's paper.

Now: This is even hard to imagine.

Then: There were no youth sports on Sundays or Sunday mornings.

Now: There's youth soccer, football, hockey and skiing, and the playfields are busy on Sunday mornings.

Then: The action was on boards and committees.

Now: The excitement is often around ministry teams.

Then: We emphasized church membership.

Now: We emphasize discipleship.

Then: Church membership and stewardship rested on a sense of obligation.

Now: Both are driven by a sense of motivation.

Then: Stewardship, at least for many, was like "paying dues."

Now: Stewardship means participation in a way of life.

Questions for Reflection and Discussion

1. What feelings did you experience as you read this series of Then and Now's?

2. Are there other Then and Now's you would add to this list?

3. Do you see these changes as positive or negative or some of both?

4. What are the most significant implications of these shifts for your church?

Resources

Books

Durall, Michael. *Creating Congregations of Generous People*. Herndon, Va.: Alban Institute, 1999. This is an excellent book that I strongly recommend for pastors and stewardship teams. Durall gets the emphasis on the right things and grounds his observations in wide experience.

Green, William C. *52 Ways to Ignite Your Congregation*. Cleveland: Pilgrim Press, 2010. Green headed stewardship for the United Church of Christ for many years. This accessible and insightful book is grounded in practical experience and a broad theological vision.

Hall, Douglas John. *The Steward: A Biblical Symbol Come of Age*. New York: Friendship Press, 1982. This book by the Canadian theologian Douglas John Hall is a comprehensive look at the symbol of the steward and stewardship as a theological key. Less about stewardship as fund development and more about it as a way of life and understanding.

Robinson, Anthony B. *Leadership for Vital Congregations*. Cleveland: Pilgrim Press, 2006. The first book in the Vital Congregations series provides an understanding of the nature and practice of congregational leadership today, for pastors, governing bodies, and lay leaders.

Robinson, Anthony B. *Transforming Congregational Culture*. Grand Rapids, Mich.: William Eerdmans Publishing, 2003. This book will help you get an overview of the new time and new challenges the church and its leaders face today.

Singer, Peter. *The Life You Can Save: Acting Now to End World Poverty*. New York: Random House, 2009. Philosopher/ethicist Peter Singer provides a look at giving and the difference we can and should be making in the global context with generous giving. Singer offers both philosophical and ethical grounds for giving as well as practical insight into where giving can help most in terms of world poverty.

Denominational Resources (United Church of Christ)

Are You Ready to Talk About Money: A Quiz A fun little booklet that helps people to get at different attitudes about money, and helps churches talk about money in a playful and humorous way. Available from United Church Resources. Great for a skit at a stewardship dinner or meeting. From the UCC Writers Group.

The Big Secret of Giving: Hidden Treasures in Life and Church, by William C. Green, 2007. This booklet offers a provocative and engaging series of short meditations on various stewardship related themes. Available from United Church Resources.

The Gifting God: Change the Way You Look at Giving, by Rochelle A. Stackhouse, United Church Resources, 2007. A fine little study for group discussions from UCC pastor and teacher Shelly Stackhouse. Available from United Church Resources.

Inspiring Generosity: A Resource of the Stewardship and Church Finances Ministry, Local Church Ministries, United Church of Christ, 2002. Prepared by William Green, Mark Suriano, and Christina Villa, this 121-page resource is the basic, current material from the United Church of Christ. The "Consecrating Stewards" program is outlined and described here, beginning on page 60.

Seasons of Stewardship: Year-Round Stewardship: A Resource for Reflection, by William Green. This eight-page resource available from Local Church Ministries helps pastors and congregations look at stewardship through all the seasons of the church year.

Notes

Chapter Two

1. Wellesley Congregational Church, United Church of Christ in Wellesley, Massachusetts.

Chapter Three

1. Michael Durall, *Creating Congregations of Generous People* (Herndon, Va.: Alban Institute, 1990), 24.

2. Peter Singer, *The Life You Can Save: Acting Now to End World Poverty* (New York: Random House, 2009), 67.

3. Barbara Brown Taylor, *Speaking of Sin: The Lost Language of Salvation* (Cambridge, Mass.: Crowley Publications, 2000), 76.

4. Ibid.

5. Ibid., 77.

6. Durall, *Creating Congregations of Generous People*, ix.

Chapter Four

1. Paul Tournier, quoted in Walter Brueggemann, *The Bible Makes Sense* (Winona, Minn.: St. Mary's Press, 1977), 59.

2. Ibid.

Chapter Five

1. Durall, *Creating Congregations of Generous People*, 24.

2. Anthony B. Robinson, *Leadership for Vital Congregations* (Cleveland: Pilgrim Press, 2007), 52.

3. Ronald H. Heifetz, *Leadership without Easy Answers* (Cambridge, Mass.: Belknap Press of Harvard University, 1994), 252.

4. Durall, *Creating Congregations of Generous People*, 15.

5. Singer, *The Life You Can Save*, 64.

6. Durall, *Creating Congregations of Generous People*, 37.

Chapter Six

1. Durall, *Creating Congregations of Generous People*, 50.

2. Durall, *Creating Congregations of Generous People*, 46.

Chapter Seven

1. William C. Green, Mark Suriano, and Christiana Villa, *Inspiring Generosity, Local Church Ministries* (Cleveland: United Church of Christ, 2004), 60–75.